MW00581091

heart is where the home is

At the end of the day, we all just want to be loved, accepted and embraced for who we are

By Vanessa Marie Dewsbury

ISBN-13: 978-1-7751949-0-3

Author: Vanessa Marie Dewsbury
vanessamariedewsbury@gmail.com

Cover Design & Layout: BrodStyles Media
Editor: Joe Mercer

Publisher: Soul Cove Publishing

dedication

This book is dedicated to everyone who believed in me.

And to those who didn't.

For my Love, my dear children, my family.

To my friends, my clients, the stranger on the street, and to anyone along my journey who has encouraged me, understood me, and has played an important role in my life.

Without you all, this dream may never have come alive as it has.

Thank you for applauding my successes. I heard you loud and clear.

disclaimer

This book is a collection of my beliefs, my perspectives, my thoughts, and my truth.

Please don't substitute my words or advice for any medical or psychiatric care that you may require from a professional physician or therapist.

Use this insight at your own discretion and with your own free will.

Perhaps our truths will align and our souls will resonate and maybe, just maybe, my words will open a place within your heart that was once closed or asleep.

It's never too late to awaken all that is within you.

my influencers

Along my journey I have been inspired by many people
who indirectly helped guide me along my path. People who have stepped
out beyond themselves and choose to take on the role of helping others
with selfless hearts and gentle souls.

Gratitude goes out to Eckhart Tolle, Wayne Dyer,
Jim Carrey, Oprah Winfrey, and Alanis Morissette.

Thank you all for sharing your truth and your beautiful light.

Vanessa's spirit is filled with love and grace. I have had the pleasure of knowing this beautiful soul for a couple of years now and have watched her live from her heart center on a daily basis. Her positive vibes radiate to those around her spreading her love and light wherever she goes.

Jen CB, *Believe In Your Dreams,* Coach, Speaker, Former Semi-Pro Athlete

I have known Vanessa for a few years now and to me, she is the real deal. She possesses a conscious willingness to walk her talk in every moment. And because of that she shines a loving light on everyone she encounters.

Ruth Garrett PhD., MSc., Author of *Who Says You Have To Be Nice?*

I have watched Vanessa evolve and expand even more into the inspirational and loving spirit she has always been. It is a great honour for me to know her as I believe her to be a Guiding Light in this we call the human experience. She reaches out with compassion and empathy to all who know her and then, to those who do not. She seems to intuit what one needs and provide it with loving accuracy. She has so many talents and gifts it does not do them justice to list them, however, I can tell you her writing has changed my life, and I know it will change yours too. Namaste.

Reverend Jessie Brandon, Metaphysical Minister

heart is where the home is

finding my way back home

My journey to becoming *lost* was gradual. So gradual, in fact, I wasn't aware I was lost, until I found home.

The home within my heart.

For many years I created and perfected masks. These masks were camouflage, a place for me to hide my truth. The fear of not being loved, accepted, and embraced for who I *really* was, forced me behind these camouflage faces.

Although I was unhappy, fearful, and suffering from anxiety, I saw myself as a butterfly in its cocoon, transitioning and preparing. I so badly wanted to spread my beautiful wings and fly.

My fears, however, kept me from breaking free, and kept me from flying.

The intention of this book is to share my experiences in hopes that some of my words resonate with you, with the truth you're living, and I hope my words help you spread your wings and fly.

When we can relate and connect with others, especially on a soul level, it brings about a feeling of comfort, safety, and hope. We all want to be understood and heard. We want our feelings to be acknowledged. We want to know we're not alone.

You are not alone.

trust in your wings

The moments we feel most lost in life often transpire before discovering who we *really* are.

It's a time when your heart and soul are seeking to align in order to find inner harmony and balance.

Not unlike the caterpillar, your transformation will take time. It will be beautiful, perfect. And it will be worth it.

Trust this process, trust your wings, and trust that you will fly.

when you shift, you shed

People.

Things.

Relationships.

Friendships.

Foods.

Habits.

Beliefs.

As you shift into alignment with your truth, you shed what no longer resonates with your heart.

Don't feel guilty, shame or regret. If we're not shifting, we're not growing.

And the purpose of life is growth.

Our masks and veils will dissolve as our beautiful souls evolve.

believing beyond reason

I believe in the magic of the Universe.

I believe we attract what we are, who we are.

I believe things happen *for us*, not *to* us.

I believe we are all worthy of happiness, health, and wealth.

I believe we all have talents, abilities, and special gifts given to us at birth.

I believe we co-create our reality with the Universe.

I believe we have within us the tools to manifest a life of bliss and abundance.

I believe we are boundless beings in a limitless Universe.

I believe in the power of our choices and how they can determine our lives.

I believe we can achieve all we dream and all we desire.

I believe if we surrender to *what is*, we can learn to accept *what isn't*, with ease and grace.

I believe at the root of all creation, is belief. If you can believe, you can receive.

aligning your journey

When we are not living authentically, we are choosing to go against what our heart desires. This can create feelings of discontentment, unhappiness, and anxiety.

Our truth is our gift. It's the very thing that makes us who we are. By hiding our truth, we hide the parts of ourselves that want to shine and be seen. For the sake of our soul, it's "spiritually important" to acknowledge every part of who we are, every layer of our being.

When putting our thoughts and energy into what makes us unhappy rather than happy, the frequency we emit is unaligned with what we truly love and what we desire.

By emitting this *unaligned* frequency, we not only attract back what we don't love, others will unconsciously feel theses inauthentic vibrations and sense our lack of genuine enthusiasm and passion in what we do.

We can remain on this resistant path or choose instead to shift our alignment to match our truth. This can take courage and perseverance, but for the health of our mind, body, and spirit, it can be the most important decision we ever make.

You can't ignore who you truly are—your truth after all, is *you.*

a soul's journey

If something lights up your heart, keep doing it. Keep feeding your soul what it loves.

We're here to experience happiness down to our core. We're here to live fully awake and boundlessly alive.

Discovering what makes you happy is a gift to yourself, to others, and to the world.

As you travel through life, be brave, bold, and relentless. Believe in yourself with all your heart and trust that what comes to you, is meant for you. Despite how it feels in the moment, it will serve you purpose in the end.

Our experiences prepare us for the next step of our journey. They make us stronger, more resilient, and build within us a wall of faith that cannot be knocked down. Deep within you is the wisdom and knowledge to help you navigate life and "grow through what you go through".

This is your one chance to live a life that pleases and satisfies your soul.

So take the road less travelled.

Be curious.

Be adventurous.

And trust that your *passion* is your *purpose*.

The moment when we have achieved true happiness is the moment we understand we don't require any "thing" to make us happy.

♥

the observer

Imagine living in a state of being where you consciously choose to *observe* rather than *absorb* what's happening around you, or you refrain from judging the character of another.

How would it feel not to view a person as "negative" but instead you just notice their energy is different from your own? Perhaps their energy is heavier because they are carrying with them trauma, pain, or hate towards self.

What if we observed without judgment and saw others as ourselves? We can become more understanding and compassionate when we see, or have seen, ourselves in others. Because we have all been there.

Sure, we don't have to accept what doesn't feel good, we don't have to spend time with people who we don't "vibe" with but I do believe that when we refer to other people as negative, it's an instant judgment when many times this "heavier" energy we feel from someone is usually coming from a hurt and angry place within their heart.

This is what holding space for others is about. It's about letting people be where they are, and meeting them there. It's the observation of a situation or person and not an engagement or entanglement of our own emotions.

Sounds pretty freeing.

To just be, as we are, and allow others to be, as they are.

accepting yourself

Be okay with where you are right now.

Accept and embrace *who* you are in this chapter of your life. Don't deny what makes you, you.

Offer your unloved parts love and your "broken" parts healing. The place you are right now is where you're meant to be until you decide to turn the page.

Whenever that shall be.

Seeking help upon this journey does not make you "weak". It makes you human, and you're doing the best you can with what you know, with what you have learned.

Love and accept yourself as you are.

Right here, right now, is where you are meant to be.

no longer ours to hold

Not everyone is ready for a new, *better* you.

As you grow closer to your true self, people are going to walk out of your life. Don't worry—it happens. Not every relationship is meant to last forever.

The truth is, as we become wiser, more connected with self, and as we learn more about who we are, some people will shift outwardly as we shift inwardly.

Attachments to many things can cause us grief and disappointment. We cannot hold onto what is no longer *ours* to hold onto.

Along the way great things come together, and even greater things may fall apart.

Nothing in this Universe is permanent, nor should it be expected to last forever. The more we try to hold onto something that's no longer meant for us, the greater the resistance we will face.

Is it time to let go of something you've been clinging to?

The gift of a new beginning could be waiting for you beyond the horizon.

When we surrender and let go of what no longer serves our souls, something even more beautiful will take its place.

When we trust what we cannot yet see, magic and miracles can happen.

illuminating our darkness

It can be daunting to face your demons, but in order to experience personal growth and self-discovery, and to heal, you must expose yourself to *every* part of you: the good, the bad, and the ugly.

Underneath the chaos and confusion muddying your mind, and between the sadness of your spirit and discontent of your heart, is a loving and kind being. The person you were born to be.

When you begin to dig deep into the depths of your soul, you will uncover the essence of who you truly are, and what was once "lost", becomes found.

we are worthy of greatness

I had a pattern of unconsciously attracting people into my life who were either unaware of their own greatness or refused to acknowledge their self-worth, and it had a tremendous effect on how they saw me.

How could they recognize *my* worth or the value of my heart when they couldn't see their own?

We are worthy of greatness, success, love, happiness, and health. It's here for us all to enjoy and experience, fully and completely. But you have to know and understand this. It's important for you to see in yourself what others may not see.

Greatness has always been there, inside you, waiting to be seen.

Love yourself more.

Find your own light and shine it brightly.

If you are surrounded by people who don't see your greatness or recognize your worth, you owe it to yourself to find the people who do.

to be okay

Some people don't want to be healed. Others have no idea they're in need of healing.

I didn't know I needed healing. I thought I was doing perfectly fine until reality shook me awake one morning and said 'you're not okay'. Despite what you tell yourself and others, *you're* not okay, *this* isn't okay. But it can be.

The darkest hours brought me my brightest light, and it was during this time that I *found* myself, healed my unloved pieces, and grew into me.

We pack away our sorrows in order to avoid the pain, guilt, or shame. But in order to heal we need to go inward and face our pain—we must *feel* it in order to *heal* it.

When you are ready, you will go within, you will face what's hiding in the corners of your heart. You will bring your darkness the light it needs, the love it desires.

Maybe you'll hear that voice telling you 'you're not okay'. Or maybe it will be your own voice you hear—'I *want* to be okay. I *need* to be okay'.

A part of you will be seeking your love.

Find that piece and touch it with compassion, love it with abandon.

beautiful hearts

Often the most beautiful stories come from once-broken hearts.

The ones who have endured pain, trauma, and tragedy, those who have experienced things one would never wish upon another.

They've wept in darkness, stood alone in the cold, but somehow they mustered the strength and courage to move forward with trust in their hearts and sheer will in their souls.

They share the light they found within themselves in hopes of helping others learn to rise and shine again.

I believe it's our shadows that teach us how to love ourselves and others more compassionately and unconditionally.

The means to our healing often resides in the darkest parts of our hearts, the parts where sadness and heartache linger and long to be seen, to be felt, to be touched by empathy.

I am grateful for those who have the courage to seek healing and for those who share their gift of love and honesty with all those who stumble upon their beautiful path.

I am thankful for the ones who turned their tragedies into triumphs.

our need for connection

We share an unconscious desire for connection. We need to relate and resonate with those around us. We yearn to find others who will listen to not only our voices, but also our hearts, our souls.

In a world full of people, it is easy to feel alone. We want to be seen, heard, and understood. We need to know that others care and they *see* us amongst the sea of others searching for the same.

Why do we crave such connection?

Because, it feels good.

We may live our lives as separate individuals, but on this earth, in this experience, and at this very moment, we are *one.*

By engaging and connecting with others, it fills us with affirmation that oneness is real.

Seek the connection you desire, the connection you crave. The act of interacting with others helps us thrive and feel alive.

*Sweet joy is found in the moments
that words just can't describe.*

♥

loving yourself

What happens when you start to love yourself? You become honest with yourself.

The more you embrace yourself as you *are*, the more you realize all the things you *aren't*.

You become empowered in your own presence, allowing yourself to refuse what doesn't serve you, and discover what does.

You begin to walk taller and feel more confident in your own skin. You become less affected by outer circumstances and the opinions of others, and you focus instead on inner awareness.

If you're walking with kindness in your step and empathy in your heart, then ultimately, nothing else matters.

When you love every inch of your soul and all parts of your heart, the truth of who you really are awakens and you start to live, fully alive.

What changes when you have true love for self, when you accept and embrace yourself just as you are?

Your entire world.

the doubt does pass

In moments of self-doubt and wavering faith, ask yourself where these thoughts are coming from.

Are they real? Are they mine? Are they authentic? Are they coming from a place of love or fear?

Your authentic self knows your value, your truth, your worth, and it knows what it loves, completely and honestly.

Your moments of self-doubt are just that, moments. Moments we have to remind ourselves not to hang onto. These too will pass.

When on a journey and path of self-creation, we put our heart and soul on the line. We become vulnerable and raw and open to judgment. We sometimes *feel* more, and *think* less.

But this path is ours to grow on. This is *our* journey. We get to spread our wings so we can soar and understand, for us, the Universe is limitless, beholding everything we need for our personal evolution.

We are living our dreams out loud because that's what we're designed to do.

Do you remember the day you discovered your gift, the day you stumbled upon something that lit up every cell in your body? Just remember that feeling during moments of self-doubt.

This is what you were called here to do, and it comes with a roller coaster of emotions. That's the joy of the ride. Every moment of vulnerability offers a chance for growth.

No one said it would be easy, but it is definitely worth it.

...and there you are

One day you wake up and wonder who you've become, where you went, and how long ago you "lost" yourself.

Your spirit seems broken, your zest and curiosity for life have faded, and you feel as though you're going through the motions, watching everyone else live their lives.

You're emotionless, yet full of emotion.

You spent years pouring your heart into everything, for everyone, and while you were busy giving your heart away, you gave *yourself* away, too.

In the process of burying your true self, you took on the labels of mother, wife, husband, friend, employee, and employer, and forgotten all the things that bring you true pleasure.

But you're so much more than a label, more than a title.

You are a nurturer, a lover, a unique creative and intelligent being who bares all with grace, and sometimes with a forced smile to protect the ones you love.

We sometimes forget this because it's been so long. But we need that friendly reminder. The reminder that there's still time to do the things you dreamed of doing. To do the things you love. To free yourself, by being yourself.

When we feel like we've lost ourselves, it often means we need to reconnect with our soul. It means it's time to go within and be selfish with our needs and gentle with our hearts.

And we need to do this without guilt or shame.

from darkness to light

I commend you for showing up as your authentic self. I respect you for allowing your vulnerable self to emerge and to be seen, especially on the darkest of days. And I admire you for living and breathing from the core of who you are, opposed to the ego self of who you *think* you are.

At some point in your life, a piece of you felt broken. You witnessed the darkness just before seeing the light. But you didn't choose to remain in the shadows, you choose instead to rise up into the light. You began to shed everything that no longer resonated with you, and you were born again into the Universe, born into your truth and undeniable love.

This is when you realized your purpose, and it was no longer a self-serving world for you. You understood fully that you are here to be of service to others, that you're here to give love and to be loved.

And from that moment you started to truly live. You started to live *in* purpose. Nothing else had ever felt better. You understood that when you're helping others, you are also helping yourself.

This is how it feels to live in the light and to give your gifts without expectations or conditions.

This is how it feels to be fully alive, to live authentically and truthfully, without a moment of doubt in your heart.

anxiety, my old friend

My message to those who suffer from anxiety: there is nothing "wrong" with you.

I've walked your journey and, at times, still do.

As an anxiety sufferer, I was often more concerned about the future than the moment I was living. And who can blame me? News outlets and social media feeds bombard us with messages of fear and unworthiness.

Disease. War. Debt. Cancer. Illness. Rejection. Hate.

The more I watched the news, the more fearful I became. I lived in constant fear, for myself, and my family. I started to believe what the television was telling me: medication was the only answer.

Of course it wasn't, not for me anyway.

My anxiety was a massive accumulation of stored stress, which became more intense when I was dealing with external triggers, health issues, or unhealthy relationships.

Most anxiety sufferers are not consciously aware of these pockets of stored stress, so it can often feel as though the anxiety spikes for no apparent reason.

When your body isn't in balance, emotionally, mentally, physically, and spiritually, stress is created. I found when I exercised, practiced yoga, meditated, and enjoyed time outdoors, my stress would dissipate. It's difficult to be stressed while immersed in nature, where we become grounded, balanced, and at peace.

Why is that? Our roots are planted in nature.

We used to chase our food, live under the sun and stars, and build our homes from what the Earth provided.

We were not meant to be planted in cubicles, on an assembly line, in front of computers, under fluorescent lighting.

It's the reason some children have trouble sitting still in a classroom all day. They were never meant to. We were built to move. It is a necessity. Our physical bodies and mental health crave it.

There are many different methods to release stress, but it starts by getting yourself moving, especially in those dark moments when it's the absolute last thing you want to do.

A ten minute walk can be like therapy. It can provide you an opportunity to change your focus and shift your attention to what better serves you.

Next, eliminate the external messages. Shut off the violence and the fear-mongering rhetoric.

When we become mindful and aware of what we allow into our consciousness, we can better control our internal messaging and state of mind.

all the little things

Abundance is grown through gratitude.

When we are thankful and grateful for everything we have in life, we become more aware of the abundance surrounding us.

From the home we are sheltered by and the food we eat, to the simple things like hitting every green light on the way to the store or the friendly neighbour who always waves hello.

When you no longer focus on what you *don't* have, you become more grateful for what you *do* have. From this state of gratefulness, more abundance is bestowed upon you.

By saying 'thank you' each day for what you have, you will create an attitude of gratitude.

As your mindset changes from a state of 'wanting more' to 'I have everything I need', you enter a place of love and appreciation, and are soon filled with a sense of peacefulness.

Take a moment to think about what makes you grateful. I promise you: the more you look, the more you'll find.

let it go

We've all been angry, feeling like we want to scream, but did you know too many of us treat anger like an all-consuming beast?

The more you *feed* it, the hungrier it gets and angrier you become.

Step back, take a deep breath.

Studies have shown the initial sensation of anger or frustration lasts, on average, 90 seconds before it begins to dissipate.

If someone cuts you off while driving to work, don't hide from the anger—experience it—just don't dwell on it. Calm yourself by breathing deeply and allow the feeling to pass.

Often times when we encounter an unpleasant situation we keep thinking about it, replaying it in our minds, telling anyone who will listen.

We can consciously and unconsciously hold onto anger, sadness, resentment, and hate, and carry it with us our entire lives.

Memories of a person or experience can cause your blood pressure to spike. That's because you have attached yourself to those feelings and emotions even though they have long passed. They actually prevent you from moving forward, from growing.

Our experiences are meant to be learning opportunities. However, we need to let them go. When we hold onto negative feelings, thoughts and emotions, they become stored in our bodies and they can eventually turn into physical pain, illness, and disease.

No one can make us feel any one way; it is a choice. And our reactions are often based on our unconscious conditioning or ingrained pain we carry with us.

We have the ability and the power to release what we no longer need and we can do this by creating a conscious connection within, and through forgiveness for self and for others.

When the seeds are planted,
those who are ready, and those
who are willing, will water them.
❤

a work in progress

We are all under construction.

We are still learning, still figuring things out, still trying to do better with what we know.

We're on different parts of the path, destination unknown, but yearning to arrive.

But what if there isn't a final destination?

What if we're always striving for the next point of arrival, only to find another?

What if we never truly *arrive*?

And if there isn't a final destination, wouldn't that mean we've already arrived?

Having already arrived doesn't mean we don't need to seek new experiences and new levels of success and happiness, it doesn't mean we stop the desire to learn, to grow, and to dream.

It means we can start to live more present and fully, in each moment knowing we have already arrived.

be authentically you

Sometimes when you express your authentic self to the world, you find the relationships you share with others will begin to change, and others will even fade away.

Why does this happen?

When you start living as your true authentic self, you soon let go of certain parts of yourself that may have resided on a lower frequency. It can be sad and disheartening when people who you've been connected to turn away, when relationships change, and perhaps end. But sometimes it's needed and it doesn't mean that there's anything wrong with you, or them, it only means that you may not resonate with that person like you once did.

That's okay. It's part of the process and evolution of your soul.

People may not understand who you've become, but keep being you, and if someone doesn't accept and embrace you, just send them love.

Never dim your magnificent light because others are afraid to shine. Don't repress the very thing the world needs more of.

Stand tall in your truth and never forsake the importance of being yourself, simply to satisfy someone else.

everything is energy

We are made of energy. It is what moves our bodies, allows us to function, and can be passed on to others as easily as we can absorb it.

We have all experienced someone walking into a room and, without even speaking, they *change* the energy. You can feel the room shift, as if the temperature dropped several degrees, and almost always, your energy soon follows. So does your mood.

Our energies interact, which is why you can meet someone and instantly like their 'vibe' (vibration), and feel drawn to them. Their presence, for no apparent reason, just feels *good*.

On the flipside, it can be very difficult when you're surrounded by lower energy people. This happens in the workplace, social environments, our own homes; it can change our state from *positive* to *negative*.

The key is to not let it.

A lack of self-awareness compounds the issue. When we're not aware of self, our behaviors, or actions, we have no problem finding fault in others and their behaviors.

To become aware of self, you need to observe how you react in situations such as the examples above. Do you immediately find the negative in most things? Do you often fault others or are quick to place blame? Do you become defensive and angry?

Many of us have *reactive* minds. Instead of observing a situation and allowing for a resolution to be found, we tend to allow our state of mind and/or emotions to dictate how we react or *overreact* to a situation.

So how do we avoid getting affected by the energies of others? Here are a few suggestions:

- Express how you feel when someone is treating you poorly. When we remain silent, it gives permission to others to treat us any way they like. Communicate how you feel and respond openly with how you would like to be treated moving forward. Set boundaries.

- Understand you are not responsible for the way others react. People like to point fingers and find blame in others instead of taking responsibility and owning their behavior. It is not *your* fault if someone reacts poorly.

- Develop self-awareness. Are you the common denominator? Do you find yourself in frequent situations where there's conflict and drama? Look within yourself and see if there's something you need to work on.

- Let go of the need to be validated. That's the need of the ego. Many people would rather be *right* than *happy*. What would you rather be?

- Do not engage or pay attention to the drama and negativity happening around you. If you stop feeding the vampire, it will go somewhere else to feast.

- If you don't feel good in an environment, don't be afraid to leave. You don't have to stay where you don't feel good.

- If you experience this is your home environment, open the doors to communication in an understanding and responsive way as opposed to a reactive and defensive manner.

- Don't take everything personally. If someone is in a foul mood and projects negativity upon you, it has nothing to do with you. Just steer clear and focus on the positive vibration you are choosing to hold.

authentic living

To live authentically means to go about your day living life from a place of pure truth.

It means speaking from your heart, trusting your intuition, and treating others the way you want to be treated.

It means removing your outer shell and no longer conforming to expectations others may have of you.

It means to breathe, and to exhale love.

When you choose to live from this glorious place that holds freedom and abundance, you undoubtedly change the quality of your life, and it can help change the lives of those around you simply by your presence.

Living authentically is when you live out your purpose, when you express all that you are from the inside, out. It's not being afraid to be vulnerable, and raw, real and true.

We can't turn back the hands of time. The only chance we have to be who we are, is right now.

People will be drawn to you through the authentic energy you produce.

be you

How do you remain visible in a seemingly overcrowded physical, social, and spiritual world?

You stand out by being you.

When you are you, truly you, you unconsciously give others permission to be themselves. This can create an instant connection and a feeling of comfort. It allows for relating and resonating to naturally occur between energies.

There seems to be no new ideas out there, everyone is doing something like you, or similar to you. To stand out, you must *live* out loud—you must express *you* from a truthful, genuine, and natural place without being influenced from external sources and energies that don't resonate with your truth.

When you present yourself to others from your authentic core, the energy exchange is powerful enough to be felt. You encompass the ability to deeply connect with the soul energy of another, and it's a magnificent thing.

Stand out, with your heart out, and radiate the energy that makes you, you.

the gift of awakening

If you are fortunate enough to experience an awakening, consider yourself blessed.

Although you will awaken to some "ugly" truths, try not to place your focus there for very long; keep moving forward as you experience the beauty of the Universe.

You will encounter unpleasant experiences with people and situations, but remember, you are blessed with internal wisdom not taught nor learned, but inside you. It helps you deal with situations and conflicts with ease and understanding.

Situations will continue to upset you and cause turmoil, but this newfound wisdom makes it much easier to accept, embrace, and move forward with the lessons learned.

It can take some getting used to, especially when you leave the *old* you and transform into the *new* you. There will be bumps and bruises along your path, but with new sight, a new perspective, and a profound feeling of gratitude for everything and everyone around you, it gets easier with time.

You'll find as you refrain from drama and dispose of negativity, you will begin to focus on the goodness within you and those around you. You'll connect more with nature and with people. You'll feel grateful for even the smallest gesture. You'll approach all things with good intentions and kindness, and without expectations, judgment, and conditions.

Growing and evolving is part of the process of awakening to oneself, to the world. You cannot control it, nor should you try. Resisting change will only stunt your personal and spiritual growth and block the new opportunities you need as a part of your life journey.

Wrap yourself in the experience of the awakening, appreciate everything, everyone, and remain humble at heart.

We give away our power
by thinking we have none.
♥

following your heart

Listen to your soul and follow your heart.

We are all born with creative and unique abilities, whether it be painting, drawing, writing, designing, singing, cooking, and the list goes on. It is what we were meant to do. It is our purpose, our passion.

It doesn't have to be a full-time career. It can be a hobby or part-time job. But what it does need to be, is fostered. If we allow that part of us to sit dormant and die, we die with it.

What do you love to do? What makes you smile? What makes you feel most alive?

Now do that.

If you don't know what drives you, meditate on it, and allow it to flow to you. Try a few different activities that may have intrigued you in the past and see what comes from that. Or try something completely new and notice how it makes you feel.

I like to say, it's in the quietest of moments that our soul speaks the loudest.

Create inner silence so you can hear what speaks to you.

let it be

Allow yourself to surrender.

Don't feel the need to control all things because in the end, the Universe has a plan, and it's always there to support you.

In the moments when you feel the disappointment of missing out on something you desired, know something greater is waiting for you.

Surrendering to, and embracing the beautiful processes of life, allows you more freedom. More opportunities will present themselves to you when you're open to receiving them.

There is no such thing as "what if". There is only "what is".

Don't worry, don't stress. Release expectations and allow events to unfold as they shall.

It's important to plan our future and to envision our dreams, but to be present in the present, you must be awake in the now.

When you're in the now, you're in the flow.

Let it be.

being still

Time spent alone with yourself is crucial and necessary in order for exceptional growth, personal evolution, and for the state of your well-being.

Our world is full of distractions and many of those distractions divert you from yourself.

When you don't allow yourself "still" time, you don't allow yourself a chance for self-reflection and inner review. You don't give your body a chance to be, and feel.

We often neglect our physical, mental, emotional, and spiritual needs, and become so disconnected from our bodies that by the end of the day, we're depleted. While our bodies are left feeling weak and tired, our minds are still working, still thinking, still worrying. The constant chatter ceases to stop.

But it's important to stop, to be still, to "Be". Our bodies send us messages all the time, and we rarely listen, but we need to. When we make it a habit to quiet our mind, the *noise* grows quiet.

When we are quiet with ourselves and take a break from the mind, we find inner wisdom, knowledge, and the valuable information that contributes to our growth and overall well-being.

It's locked up inside of us and only we hold the key.

To be "still" creates a mind and body connection that our spirit yearns for.

Be still, feel, listen.

be the change

If you want to change your life, you will have to change your mind.

If your external circumstances, situations, and relationships aren't making you content, it's up to you to make changes.

We often wait for external circumstances to change in order for us to be happy. We expect others to make changes to please us. Or we remain comfortably numb, enduring unhappiness.

What we sometimes fail to realize is that the fountain of happiness flows only through us.

Our bodies, minds, and souls are in a constant state of change. When we're resistant to that change, the flow is disrupted, and discontentment and unhappiness begins to bog us down.

Life isn't supposed to always be hard. The hard times we do experience act as lessons, providing us with an opportunity for wisdom and growth. But hard times aren't meant to stay.

Once you accept that something needs to change, you can then decide to handle your situation differently.

Your energy and your thoughts affect your environment. What you think about, you become.

Internal awareness will change everything.

Be the change.

a commendable being

Do you know what is truly commendable?

The act of being able to have a respectful, civilized, and decent conversation with someone whose beliefs and opinions don't align with your own.

We've all seen complete strangers name-calling, bullying, and spewing words of hate and anger, all because they don't share the same view.

But there is something much deeper going on below the surface of a person who feels the need to always be right. Something they need to address and conceivably heal.

A person who holds inner peace does not feel the need to prove others wrong, or to project hate and anger.

Unfortunately, peace isn't always easy to find or hold onto. The day-to-day stressors of today's world can cause inner conflict that tarnishes our abilities to be okay with ourselves and with others.

Everyone is fighting an inner battle. Some have unearthed the tools to properly handle the impacts of these conflicts, while others become overwhelmed by their feelings.

Understanding that there is more than meets the eye allows for compassion toward others, and makes it easier to share your peace.

clarity is power

When it comes to manifesting your physical reality, you must be specific with the details in order to achieve what you desire.

Relationships: What do you seek in a partner? What will fulfil you, emotionally, mentally, physically, and spiritually? These four pillars help build a stable foundation for a healthy relationship. If you don't know what you desire, you will seek partners who fail to fulfill your needs, and vice versa, leading to breakdowns in the relationship.

Career: What do you see yourself doing? What makes you happy? What brings you enjoyment? What makes you want to jump out of bed in the morning? Write it down. Then write down where you see yourself in five years, ten years, twenty. Make sure you focus on detail, because, as they say: it's all in the details. Find that thing that makes your spirit soar and your soul content.

Friendship: What kind of friends are you attracting into your life? Are the friendships you're forming worthy of your time, effort, and energy? Have you been clear about the kind of people you want to surround yourself with? Are you specific about how you want to be treated and respected? Are boundaries being crossed because you haven't been clear?

A life is built and you hold the blueprints.

Be precise, be the architect, and create your own life.

a time to change

How do you know when you need to make a change?

Because something isn't working. Because things seems hard and unbearable and you can't take it anymore. That's how you know when change is required.

We can become so comfortable in our current situation that pain becomes normal and accepted. It becomes a way of life. So we talk about the pain, but don't take action.

Life wasn't meant to be hard. Yes we have hard times, but those hard times are what pushes and initiates change. Take a long, hard look at your past experiences: what were your hardest most painful times? What came from those experiences?

Change.

Whether it was leaving an unfulfilling job or unhealthy relationship, the hard times led to difficult decisions.

When we're struggling it's not because we're doing something wrong, it's because change is required in some form or another. We can't fear change. It happens without our consent, every single moment. What we need to do is understand that we're *always* changing. That is why resisting change and life's natural occurrence leaves us feeling anxious, fearful, depressed, and unhappy.

So what does one do? Realize you're experiencing your current situation for a reason—some aspect of it needs to change. Ignoring it will only make it worse. Make a plan, take responsibility, and own it.

If you need to seek guidance as to how to go about change, confide in someone you trust.

Many times we know something needs to change, we just don't know how to go about it.

Recognizing it is a great start.

change yourself and the people around you will change

I remember a time when I wanted to change the world.

It was my mission.

Then somewhere along the way I realized I wasn't going to be able to do that. Not the way I thought I could anyways. I soon understood that in order to help change the world, I needed to change myself. I needed to start at the root—*me*—and my being.

I needed to grow and nurture my own soul so it could grow strong. Strong enough that it could be shared with everyone and everything.

I had to find my true self, to ensure my intentions for myself and others came from a genuine place within my heart.

The key to helping change the world starts internally, but the result is felt externally.

Share your light, your love, inspire others, and give graciously, openly, honestly, and tenderly.

Change begins within.

*As we progress throughout
our lives and form new friendships
along the way, it becomes more about
the quality of the people who we choose
to spend time with, the quantity soon
ceases to matter. I'd rather have one friend
of quality than five friends without.*

♥

tides of change

Change is inevitable. It happens without notice and without warning. It's something we can't stop nor slow down, just like time.

But what we sometimes do is choose not to accept change when change is needed. Therefore we deny the growth and opportunities that accompany change.

There are people who are satisfied remaining uncomfortably comfortable, even if it means misery and discontent. And there are those who choose the act of being uncomfortable to get comfortable. They adapt and welcome the winds of change with only faith and hope to hold on to.

The most beautiful change occurs when you dive into the layers of your authentic being and swim through the waves of your perfect soul, facing the uncertainty with trust and belief that all can be, and will be well.

When embracing change it often means everything you once held tightly, falls apart. However, in order for new, better things to come together, we need those things to fall apart.

Don't fear change because it holds the unknown, instead seek the gift and new beginning that may await you.

Sometimes things need to be "broken" in order to be fixed.

money is energy

Many people have an unhealthy relationship with money.

This relationship can lead to limiting behaviors and distorted views, some of which can result in financial hardships and ill intentions.

For a very long time I lived with a mindset of scarcity. I would frequently tell myself, others, and the Universe that I didn't have money or *enough* money.

Once I understood that money is a form of energy used for the exchange of services, I started to develop a healthier relationship with money and grew a mindset of abundance. Even when my funds were low, I envisioned them as plentiful.

I even changed my language toward money. Now when I purchase a product or pay for a service, I say I'm *circulating* my money, (not spending it) because I know it will come back to me, full circle.

Money is the form of energy we use to help pay for our warm homes, the food we eat, the experiences we indulge in with our families, and the trips to hot and sunny places that provide memories that last a lifetime.

Money is also the currency we use to help others.

Although Mother Teresa passed away in 1997, her charity continues to receive monetary donations from around the globe. Why? For nearly seventy years, the Nobel Prize winner vowed to live in poverty while using the millions of dollars she accumulated to help change the lives of so many in need.

Your thoughts, beliefs, and language will shape your relationship with money.

Do what you must to ensure those beliefs are not limiting.

filling our children with love

Don't forget to fill your children's hearts with love, confidence, words of praise, and soulful compliments.

Don't forget to make them feel safe, happy, loved, and appreciated.

Commend them on their accomplishments, especially the little things. Compliments go a long way.

You need to fill the part of their soul that seeks affirmation, the part that wants to know you care.

If we don't give to our children what they emotionally need, they will unconsciously find a way to fill that void.

Foster their confidence, their self-esteem, and be their endless fountain of love. Your children are beautiful, intelligent, creative, and unique. They need to hear that from *you.*

If they hear it from you, they can learn to hear it from themselves.

If nothing is missing, they have nothing to look for.

beneath it all

Do you know what is amazing? The act of embracing others in a genuine, heartfelt, and loving hug.

A timeless moment that allows you to feel truly connected to another.

Labels, beliefs, genders, religions, skin colour all appears to separate us, but we are not separate.

We are one.

We may have different personalities, qualities, talents, and unique abilities, but beneath it all, we are souls seeking connection.

Embrace another, breathe in the connection, feel the love.

breaking free from within

Many people have told me they feel *unsettled* in life, as though a piece of them is missing, and they are overwhelmed with the inclination to escape.

I am no stranger to this feeling—I've lived through it many times.

I knew, in my bones, that I wasn't following the path that was best for me, that I was supposed to be doing something else. Only, I didn't know what that *something* was.

I was overcome with a desire to escape, not my life, but the unsettled feelings.

After several attempts at finding my way, I discovered what I loved and began following my heart. The feeling soon diminished as my truth began to align with my higher self.

It is hard to see it when you're in the moment, but these unsettled feelings are a blessing in disguise. It means your body and mind are in tune with your soul and are relaying messages to you.

By being aware of this, it means you can act on the feeling, get to know it, understand it and realize there's something inside you trying to break free and come alive.

Finding a creative outlet, meditating, or healing therapies can help you discover your purpose.

So listen to your body when it's trying to tell you something, sink into the unsettling feelings for it might just be your gift calling you home.

let your true self shine

At times we can lose connection with our true self.

Whether it is from conditioning, doing what we are told, or the expectations others have of us, many of us go through life thinking we have to follow a path that isn't our own.

Living life this way suppresses our true self, our pure authentic being. It can then cause anxiety, depression, stress, guilt, and resentment toward others and ourselves.

However, we don't always understand why we're feeling this way. We consciously *assume* it's stemmed from an outside influence or source. But this feeling is coming from inside, a place within your core, your inner source.

It is the result of hiding your true self, your inner most deep desires, and it's caused by failing to follow your heart.

Your true self wants to be seen.

Allow yourself to be seen.

Allow yourself to shine.

follow the pull

Follow the pull of your heart and avoid, if you can, the need to push away that which resists.

How can you tell when something is designed and destined to be? You feel an internal pull, an excitement, a motivation that inspires you to follow the pull effortlessly with curiosity.

When you are forcing yourself down a path that isn't meant for you, it is draining, time consuming, and often ends in heartache or disappointment. Listen to that the hesitation you hear in your heart, it is trying to guide you home.

We do this in relationships, friendships, business, careers, in many aspects of our lives. Sometimes our minds tell us we need to push against the grain to gain control. But what isn't meant to be, isn't meant to be.

Wade into the ocean. Be taken by the waves and quiet the urge to swim against the current. It's much easier to allow what's meant to be, than to try and control what isn't.

Follow the pull, it contains your truth.

the magic of the universe

When I think of magic, I think of the *little* things in life.

A sunset on a warm summer night.

I think of the sounds of loons as they drift upon the water, their voices echoing through the darkness.

I think of the laughter with friends and family, where in that moment, all is truly well.

Magic can be felt by recognizing, appreciating, and being grateful for the beautiful gifts life has given us.

When you believe in magic, you'll begin to see it and feel it everywhere you go.

Do you believe in magic?

who are you?

I'm not asking your name or the labels you've accepted or how you think others define you. I'm curious about *who* you are, deep inside, beneath the layers and amidst the fears.

I'm curious about what makes your soul soar, what makes you laugh, and what makes your heart break.

I'm intrigued by what makes you wonder, yearn for more, what pulls you, and what pushes you. I would love to know what makes up the parts of you and, mostly importantly, I want to know, are you happy? Are you good?

Are you following your dreams, enjoying the things you love, are you going to bed at night with a pleased soul and a joyful heart?

Dig into *who* you are. *Dig deep.*

I want to know all the things that make you dance, the moments that bring you to tears.

I want to know who *you* are.

*Belief is the root
of all creation.*

♥

happiness is an inside job

The magic of the Universe can be experienced when we allow ourselves to fall into the flow of what *is* as opposed to the resistance of what *isn't*.

Once we surrender and allow the flow to do its thing, we can experience true freedom, grace, abundance, and *magic*.

Magic comes from appreciating and acknowledging the abundance we're experiencing in our everyday lives and understanding that true, everlasting happiness is 100 per cent an inside job.

When we stop seeking external happiness from others and realize we are responsible for our own happiness, we begin to understand that things happen *for* us, not *to* us.

Our experiences are required for growth.

If we don't experience the bad, how will we recognize the good?

the beauty of journaling

The art of daily journaling not only inspires inner creativity, but also releases unwanted "lower" energy and thoughts you may have experienced throughout the day.

Journaling offers you the opportunity for the self-reflection of your personal growth and development, and allows you to observe your moods, feelings, emotions, and experiences in relation to your current journey.

It's easy to lie to yourself when it's just you and your thoughts, but putting your words on paper can help you clear your mind of the clutter and see the truth.

The art of writing is, in itself, cathartic. It can help lessen stress, anxiety, and depression, and heighten inner peace. It can open your mind and heart, help heal old wounds, and provide a safe place where dreams soar and your imagination roams free.

limited beliefs

Limited beliefs are beliefs we have about ourselves and others.

They can prevent and even stop us from living out our full potential by not allowing us to recognize our own worth and capabilities. And they do quite well at limiting what we think, or *don't* think we can achieve in life.

A lot of the beliefs we hold about ourselves and others are simply borrowed beliefs. They became embedded in our unconscious mind throughout our life.

So how does one change their limiting belief system?

By rewiring our brains.

Start by identifying a limited belief that may be holding you back, for example, 'I don't have what it takes to start my own business'.

Choose instead to believe that you *are* a capable entrepreneur. Get rid of your limited belief by replacing it with a reaffirming and positive belief.

If you feel you're not worthy of a happy relationship, remind and assure yourself that you *are*. You can state, 'I am worthy of happy and healthy relationships'.

Meditations are very helpful for this process and there are many amazing videos on YouTube that can help you rewire your brain and fill it with new, positive, and "unlimited" beliefs.

'I AM' statements are also a beneficial way to help change your views and ingrained beliefs.

Make a list of all the limited beliefs you have. Beside them write the opposite belief. Look at the list often and become more aware and mindful of your self-talk—because what we tell ourselves, we believe.

How wonderful it is to know and *believe* we possess the power and the tools to change our limited belief system, allowing us to become more empowered and in control of our lives.

our hearts on the line

As a creative being, we put ourselves on display every day and take the risk of potential judgment and rejection.

Because many of us see our work as a reflection of ourselves, we often take criticism personally. It's hard not to. You've poured your heart onto a page or canvas or into a project. It is part of you. An expression from your soul.

A wise woman once told me: "once you create something and put it out there, release the expectations."

Not everyone will appreciate or like what you do, but that's just the way the world works, and that's perfectly okay.

It is also important to remember that criticism, if delivered with your best interests at heart, can be a gift. It can assist in your growth as an artist and provide you with the tools you need to perfect your craft.

Put your heart on the line, and release the expectations.

each day is an opportunity

As the author of our own story, we awake every morning with the opportunity to create our day.

Begin by making a list of what you'd like to accomplish. Big and small. Not all accomplishments are moonshots. Set the bar low and step over it. Accomplishments equal confidence.

When you make a list of what you would like to complete any given day, you become more proactive in the process of creating your day.

What's even more amazing is that you can create your entire life!

Using visualization to reach your larger, long-term goals has been proven to be very beneficial. Take some time every day: five, ten, fifteen minutes and visualize *where* you want to be, *when* you want to be there, and *how* you will *feel* when you achieve what it is you wish to create into physical reality.

The Universe does not know the difference between reality and fiction, so visualize your goals and dreams like they have already manifested.

Remember: everything in your life requires intention and action—nothing is done without either.

It is time to become a conscious creator of your reality.

sometimes life gets in the way

The distractions of life can consume you and take you away from the things that truly matter.

You may try to convince yourself that you're doing your best, but something deep inside knows 'I can do better than this'.

Discovering what's important, not only for you, but for everyone you love, is key to developing and maintaining healthy relationships.

When you remove you, from *your*self, you begin to see life in a new light.

Distractions will dance around you. They will be intriguing and persistent, yet deceitful and dishonest, and make it easy to get caught up and lost in what you *think* is working.

Watch for the little reminders telling you it's not.

Distractions create a disconnect, from you, and from those around you.

Do you want to make someone feel important, really important? Give them *all* of your attention.

The time you give to others is priceless.

just look around you

If you ever think your dreams can't come true, look around you.

Everything you see and touch started out as an idea. It derived from imagination and belief, a dream that was nurtured and loved.

Start believing in yourself, your ideas, your abilities, your visions.

Dreams can come true when you dare to believe in them.

So believe in yourself with all of your heart.

our gifts at birth

We are born with a gift inside us.

It can take years to find, decades even, but if you search for your internal treasure, your unique gift, you'll find it.

Once you discover it, the only person who can stop you from using your gift and sharing it with the world is *you*. The only obstacles you'll ever face, are the obstacles you create for yourself.

Your gift is your unique talent, it's your purpose, your passion. It's the thing that you get lost in, the thing that makes you lose track of time. It's the one thing that makes you truly happy.

When we were children we played. We created and discovered and learned something new each day. We were curious and adventurous and had no fears, and we were often relentless and stubborn and wanted to do things our own way. We never got tired of playing because we were doing what we love, and you can never tire from doing what you love.

Discover your inner child and find your gift, and be brave enough and bold enough to share it with the world.

You are worthy of every dream you hold.

*Your authenticity is part
of your brand. Show up as your
authentic self and those who
need you, will always find you.*

♥

our gifts at birth (part 2)

For those who have chosen to follow your dreams and not work your typical 9-to-5 day job, you are not lazy, or uneducated, or a burden to society.

You are choosing to live a life that makes *you* happy.

You've decided that it's more important for you and your family to be happy rather than being someone you're not meant to be, someone who others may think you *should* be.

Living a life that doesn't suit your inner needs is spiritual suicide. It's going against your own truth and denying yourself *real* happiness.

So continue to follow your heart, for it always knows the way.

shine brightly, even in the shade

Someone once said to me that they were tired of me always talking about the importance of living your dreams and encouraging others to do the same.

In the past, reading those words from someone, especially someone so close to me, would hurt my heart. They would sting my soul and impale my spirit.

However, this time the *hurtful* words didn't hurt at all. I didn't feel the need to defend myself or justify my beliefs. I didn't get offended or bent out of shape. I remained in my space as the observer instead of choosing to entangle my emotions and feelings into someone else's perception.

Their words were not *because* of me, they were only *about* me. They were merely an opinion. Since my awakening I have learned that people's opinions of me are none of my business.

Their words didn't dampen my dreams, they fuelled my fire, and I grew more relentless and passionate. I realized that for every one person who didn't believe in me, there were 100 people who did.

I came to the realization that dream-chasing isn't for everyone, and perhaps what may not appear as an ideal *dream* life to me, doesn't mean it isn't for them. Every dream is different.

More importantly, I learned no matter what someone's opinion is of me, I'll never let it dim my light. I will keep sharing my thoughts, spreading inspiration, and planting my seeds.

I am not here to hide in the corner, I am here to speak and share my truth.

And I am here to shine my brilliant light into the darkness of the world.

creating your own path

I've never been one to follow the beaten path; it seemed too mundane and boring for me.

I have chosen instead to blaze my own path, to dream my own dreams, and because I follow my own heart's path, it has led me to a life of freedom.

A life of peace and a life of love.

My path has been riddled with heartache, sadness, and gut-wrenching pain. It definitely hasn't been easy, but it was necessary, and it was needed for the growth of my soul and the revelation of my truth.

I needed my pain, my hurt, and my sorrow to make me what I am today. From the anguish, I grew into who I was meant to be.

Never fear your path, trust the curves and the crevices. It won't be easy, but it will surely be worth it.

creating your own path (part two)

Did you get ready for a job today you don't like? Did you drag yourself out of bed and tackle the commute, only to watch the clock, waiting for the day to end before it even begins?

Is there something you'd love to do but fear breaking free from the *comfort* offered by your *secure* job?

Brave are the ones who, at some point, decided there's more to life than working 9-to-5 until you can afford to retire.

You have to learn to say *yes* to your life, *yes* to your dreams, and *yes* to your future. You were not put on this earth to work your fingers to the bone for someone else; you are here to live your dreams, to enjoy this miracle of life, and to create success—not measured by dollar signs you accumulate in your bank account, but by the amount of happiness you have in your heart.

Life is about growth, you must be willing to go forward and face your fears again and again and again until they become a part of your past. There's a difference between having a fear, and fear having you. Don't let it imprison you and keep you from true happiness.

If you don't know what you truly desire and you feel an emptiness inside in your current situation, explore your inner being and see what you unearth.

The answers are inside you, waiting to be discovered.

empathetic at heart

Empathy is having the ability to understand another's emotions.

It's being able to relate, connect, and acknowledge another's experience, without experiencing the moment firsthand.

Empathy is a true gift built within one's heart. It's possessing the ability to care and love outside of your own needs.

However, empathy can breed pain. As an empathic being, you can be greatly affected by the negative experiences you encounter. The key is to not absorb the negative emotions from the perceived experience but rather, to remain as an observer. Don't be attached to the experience; attachment can cause unnecessary pain.

If you are an empathetic being, take time for yourself whenever you feel overwhelmed by the hardships of others. It's important to disconnect from the external world in order to replenish your internal world.

When you take the time to refill your glass, everyone benefits.

nothing to worry about

If someone doesn't *like* you, don't waste your time trying to figure out why.

Don't lose sleep or energy because of it.

Not everyone clicks, not everyone jives, not everyone will feel a connection with you, and guess what…they don't have to.

Sometimes energies don't match and frequencies don't align. That's just how this thing called life works.

However, when you focus your energy on someone who doesn't like you, you're taking away energy and precious time from those who do. Energy goes where your mind flows, so be mindful of where you want it to go.

Living a false life to satisfy others will leave you feeling hollow and unfulfilled.

Instead, focus on the people in your life who love you for you. Every wrinkle, every scar. They can help you see your many gifts, your talents, and your strange little quirks that make them smile.

It may end up being that nudge (if you need it) toward learning how to love yourself a little more.

life's bliss

Life can be serious but shouldn't be taken too seriously.

Stressing over every small detail, overanalyzing every comment and opinion, and striving to amass physical belongings is the opposite of living.

Life isn't about who has the biggest house or the nicest car. Life is about experiencing the beauty in the gifts we were given. It's about eating the foods we enjoy. It's dancing in the rain, watching a sunrise, listening to your favorite song on repeat, or getting lost in a book. It's the sound of birds in the morning, a smile, a tear, the feeling of a loved one's hand pressed tightly in our own.

It's about thriving and living and loving, and appreciating the company of those around us. It's about making new connections and fostering the old ones.

It's about dreaming, giving, having compassion, empathy, and showing kindness.

Be you. Be love. Be generous. Be thankful.

Accept what was. Surrender to what is.
Trust what is to come. And always, always,
follow your beautiful heart.

♥

feel the fear, but don't feed it

Many of us have lingering fears and worries that haunt us.

They take up residence in our minds and prevent us from taking risks, from loving, from living.

They creep up on us when we least expect them and cause us to have moments of self-doubt and hesitation.

But no matter how much fear you carry in your heart or how much you worry about your current or impending situation, the outcome cannot be altered by it.

Fear is a useless weapon. It has no *real* power. We give it its strength by the thoughts we feed it.

If it is true we have nothing to fear but fear itself, by recognizing when it arrives, we can then allow it to pass. If it is capable of *arriving*, it is capable of *departing*.

Fear and worry can come from unconscious pockets within us that hold onto unpleasant experiences that once caused us pain, grief, or suffering.

If we can learn to embrace, endure, and even accept fear for what it is, then we can overcome most anything that comes our way.

every moment is now

I am fuelled by spontaneity, living moment to moment.

This has enabled me to deal with situations with more grace, and has given me the ability to think quickly and make rational decisions.

It has allowed me the freedom to carry less attachments to things and people. It has ousted the feelings of disappointment due to my lack of expectations, both of myself and of others.

It has created a less stressful environment filled with excitement, adventure, and curiosity. I have adopted, without forethought, a Zen way of living. In turn, I live in peace and with an abundance of love, gratitude, and contentment.

I don't disagree with planning ahead—at times it's necessary—but I am always ready to embrace every opportunity that glances my way.

Life is at its best when you accept and forgive the past, and sink into the present. Time is just a tool, take away the clocks, and every moment folds perfectly into the next.

Every moment is now, and that's all we really have.

did you choose to be happy today?

Who else woke up today and decided, regardless of what happens, today will be a good day?

Whatever *difficulties* you encounter, face them with hope and trust, with compassion and love.

Whatever obstacles are waiting to meet you, give them your attention and patience.

Whatever situation doesn't flow with your own, find your tolerance within.

Whatever negativity may surround you, breathe out your positivity.

And any emptiness you may feel, remember the abundance at your fingertips.

The moment we choose the power of choice is the moment we are free.

are you god?

What if *you* are God?

What if everything inside of you and everything outside of you is God? The water, the trees, the animals, the skies, the entire Universe.

What if after all this time, your search for God was meant to be done inwardly?

What if you need to believe in *you*? What if it's you who deserves your utmost worshiping, honor, and respect? What if your faith only needs to be in yourself, and it is *you* who has the answers?

What if it's *you* who possesses the power to answer your own prayers? What if nature is the church you need to visit and, in its solitude and silence, you hear God—you hear yourself?

And within *you*, you find God.

I believe in a higher power, an intelligent creator who designed this perfect Universe, and I believe we are all part of this conscious creation.

We are what we have come from.

We are God, and God is Us.

sharing love and gratitude

While riding my bicycle one Sunday morning I passed an older gentleman who looked a lot like Santa Claus.

He called out to me and told me he liked my bike, and that it was beautiful, and so was I. He then wished me a wonderful day. I returned the gesture and pedaled on.

In the past, when I was more focused on myself, I would have come away from the conversation hearing only: "it's beautiful, just like you".

Instead I found myself thinking about how content and happy the man was, and how he must love his life.

Why?

I could tell he was grateful. When you become grateful of what you've been given, and all that is around you, you can't help but express this through kind words and actions. It becomes natural and easy to speak to strangers and listen, *really* listen, to what they have to say.

I share kind words and compliments with anyone, anywhere, because I feel good, and I want others to feel good as well.

Be grateful for everything you have, even the tiniest moments that bring you happiness. From within this place comes peace and unconditional love, both of which you can't help but share with others.

When you stop focusing on what you don't have and shift your focus, you soon appreciate everything you do have, and you become more aware of the needs of others.

choose your thoughts wisely

You can't be happy and unhappy at the same time.

The only way you can change states of happiness to unhappiness is by choosing your thoughts.

Positive or negative thoughts.

Happy or unhappy thoughts.

You decide your thoughts, you decide your state of mind.

While circumstances can affect your current state of mind, the duration of the effect is ultimately *your* decision.

Do you remain affected by external elements and allow them to internally effect and control you, sometimes permanently? Or do you allow them to flow through you without the need of attachment to the emotion?

We need to experience pain and hurt, it's part of the process of life. We don't, however, need to hold onto thoughts that don't serve a positive purpose.

Consciously release any thoughts that stunt your spiritual growth.

you can get through this

To those who are struggling with something in this very moment, know that in every burden, there is a blessing.

Perhaps it's hard to see right now or understand during this process, but you will eventually look back upon this day and realize you survived, just like you have in every situation you've faced before.

This is a time to feel, to listen, and to cry if you need to. What is happening right now is needed for your own growth and soul development.

Remember, nothing truly ends, it just flows and grows into another new beginning.

you hold the key

I figured out the secret to life.

The secret is, there is *no* secret.

When we search for what unlocks the doors to happiness and contentment, satisfaction, and abundance, we often seek and search externally.

But the *key*, not the *secret*, is within you.

The key to happiness is understanding, without a doubt, that only *you* are responsible for your happiness. It is purely an inside job. It is knowing you don't have to wait for happiness or achieve it from an external sources.

Authentic happiness is living in the current moment and being fully satisfied with what that moment brings.

True happiness is a state of mind. When we experience feelings of sadness, anger, hurt and pain, those feelings are often temporary. Once we choose to live in a state of happiness, those feelings cannot stagnate unless we choose to hold onto them and allow them to alter our state.

Until you reach an understanding that happiness is created within oneself, you will continue to seek happiness elsewhere.

But it begins within.

It begins with you.

healthy food, healthy mind

A healthy body is essential in maintaining a healthy mind.

The food we put into our bodies influences *every* aspect of our lives: it affects how we feel, how we think, and how we function.

Dead foods, such as refined grains and sugars, contain little or no nutritional value, keep your energy low, and can lower your vibration.

This is an avoidable burden many of us place upon our bodies. This can cause a lack of motivation, promote imbalances, and lead to degenerative diseases.

Being mindful of what we consume benefits not only the health of our physical body, but the health of our emotional, mental, and spiritual elements as well.

Live foods make you feel alive.

Eat good, feel good.

how are you?

I was in a seven-year relationship with a man who never asked me, "how are you?"

It dawned upon me one day how important that question is, and how sad it was that he never asked.

Then I felt sad for *him.*

He was never taught the importance of that one simple question. A question that says, without saying, "I care about you", "I care about how you feel", and "I want to know how you're feeling".

I can only assume the ones he loved the most never asked him.

When we grow up not knowing how to show love or emotional support to our loved ones, we lack the empathy and capacity to know how when we're adults.

However, we have a choice to change how we've been conditioned. All of us are clever enough to know what someone needs—because we usually need the same thing.

It's just one simple question, but it can change a life.

don't believe everything you think

The moment I truly started to heal was the moment I realized I wasn't sick in the first place.

Our brains can trick our bodies in many ways—from placebo pain medication to hysterical blindness and false pregnancy—proving that what you *think* about your health, truly matters, because our bodies listen to what they're being told.

It is the reason why some terminally ill cancer patients survive and others do not. Clinical studies have shown that it is possible to boost your immune system by believing you can. The survivors believed the treatment they chose, whether it was chemotherapy or holistic medicine, was going to work.

I speak with my unconscious mind all the time and ask it to heal what ails me. And many times it has listened and complied.

Changing your mindset can be easy. Instead of thinking or stating 'I *have* allergies', for example, tell yourself 'I'm currently *experiencing* allergies'. And view it as only a temporary, not a permanent experience.

Our minds are more powerful and influential than we could possibly imagine, so be mindful of what you tell it.

you're always on the right path

Are you on the right path?

The short answer is absolutely.

Even when the path feels *wrong*, you're going in the *right* direction. The experiences we encounter, the good and the bad, are necessary for our growth and development.

The lessons they provide arm us with the tools and knowledge we require as we continue along our journey.

There have been many times in my life where I could have thought I was on the *wrong* path, but those unpleasant experiences led me to where I am today.

Even though it won't feel like it at the time, the challenge is knowing and believing that our failures and mistakes will provide us with tremendous learning opportunities.

It is up to us what we do with those lessons.

If you listen closely in these situations, your unconscious will suggest to you that perhaps it's time for a change. This is when you must go within for self-reflection and to see what you can do differently.

Our higher self is always looking out for our best interests. It's the little voice in the back of our mind that tries to steer us in the right direction when we are making choices that don't align with us spiritually, mentally, emotionally, or physically. It's our inner guidance system and intuitive wisdom looking out for us.

Engage each day with an attitude of positivity and gratitude, and follow your path with trust, and believe that every step is a step toward your truth.

no more waiting

If you are waiting for life to happen *for* you rather than going out and finding the opportunities that await, you'd had better not hold your breath.

Nothing happens in this universe without intention and action.

The only person in control of that, is *you*.

A dear friend of mine was recently faced with a life-changing choice. Remain in a job that made him unhappy and unfulfilled, but paid the bills. Or walk away from the only career he had ever known, sell his home, and leave his friends behind, to move several hours away to be with the man he loved.

After toiling over his decision for some time, my partner finally sat down with him and asked him a single question.

What do you want to have written on your gravestone?

Tireless worker?

Or a man who followed his dreams and chose love?

He's since given his notice and is enjoying a life of love and happiness. A life he almost gave away.

Seek your desires, play out your passions, and face the fears that try to prevent you from unveiling and living your truth.

acts of kindness

Random acts of kindness shouldn't be *random*.

These acts should be part of who you are and what you do, every single day. Acts of kindness with the intention of love is beautiful and heartfelt, and can turn someone's day around in an instant.

You are helping conquer darkness one act at a time.

The trick is, don't allow your ego to be involved. Don't go looking for a pat on the back. Do it through genuine love and true desire to help others.

Not only will a random act give your soul satisfaction, it produces a ripple effect that will reach others; there is no way of knowing how far and wide your one act will carry.

That's the magic about it.

Practice these acts of kindness until they no longer feel *random* and they become a part of who you are.

After the rain, comes the rainbow.
All storms will pass and bring you
new light. Experience the storm
and await the rainbow.
♥

it's human nature to judge

We make judgments all the time, both consciously and unconsciously.

How you perceive an action or person is altered by opinion, both your own and those taught to you, education or ignorance, and any feelings you may have toward that action or person.

When you find yourself judging another, ask yourself where the judgement is originating.

Is it yours or are you allowing others to highjack your thoughts and emotions?

Is it your ego?

Is it learned behavior?

It is important to understand that when judging an action or a person, you are judging yourself and what you *do* and *don't* accept about yourself.

How many times has a family member or friend gone out of their way to comment on a mutual acquaintance's behavior or actions and, during the conversation, you realize the *judge* is "guilty" of the same offences?

Judgement of others is the most valuable mirror you can own. It offers a form of personal reflection not found anywhere else.

What do you see?

offer love

The world isn't always a pretty place. There is destruction, hate, war, death, and more sadness then we could ever imagine.

Remaining positive, uplifting, encouraging, generous, and authentic in your heart is one of the greatest gifts you can give, not only to yourself, but the rest of the world.

When you share words that come from a loving place in your heart, you share the peace within you, and the effects flow like rivers, touching everyone you encounter, washing over their souls, bringing love to their lives.

When you share love, you share your light.

When you help light the way, you give hope to others.

a life of learning

Not everyone is going to like me, and I don't expect them to.

I know I can't please all people, all of time, but if I'm kind, giving, and loving, then I can say I did my best.

And that's enough for me.

I've learned I won't connect with everyone I meet. My energies may not resonate with all whom I come into contact with, but that's the Ying and Yang and beauty of life. I don't need to understand *why*, I just need to understand it's going to happen, and that it's perfectly okay.

If I am irritated or triggered by another's actions or words, then I must look within me; it is there that I will find the source of my feelings or frustrations.

In order to grow, I need to experience pain. Without pain to push me, I stay stagnant and complacent, and miss an opportunity to learn.

I've discovered that although *they* say people can only hurt you if you allow them, for this to be true, your heart would have to be made of stone. Words and actions can hurt. However, how long they hurt is up to you; it is a matter of personal choice.

Do I hang on or let it go?

I've learned that things happen *for* me, not *to* me. If I believed life happened *to* me and *against* me, I would be a victim. By understanding life happens *for* me, I embrace the mentality of a survivor, a warrior, someone who gets back up, someone who doesn't give in.

I've learned the world is full of noise. The noise of distractions, negativity, anger, and evil.

I've also learned that if I live in the darkness of the noise and allowed it to tuck me in every night, then I will have learned nothing at all.

our magical existence

I ran around the block tonight a couple of times while the beautiful and peaceful snow was falling.

It felt amazing. I felt fully alive.

I allowed the gentle flakes to fall upon my face and rest on my eyelashes as I looked up into the endless sky and imagined all the other planets out there, light years away. I wondered *who* or *what* resided on those planets, and I found myself wondering what their life was like.

In that moment I felt very small, almost insignificant in comparison to the vast Universe yet, as my heart beat strongly in my chest, I felt bigger than *who* I am and *what* I am.

I felt the connection.

We are one, from the same source, created from love.

Whether you are sad, overwhelmed, and angry or happy and content, step out your door, look up, and think: I'm alive, I'm here, I'm part of this magical miracle, and I'm going to do everything in my power to embrace and appreciate this beautiful experience.

the root of anger

Anger is a symptom of unhealed wounds.

Beneath the surface, you'll discover the root.

In order to remove the root, you'll have to dig deep.

Within the roots of our anger, lies the pieces of you that require your attention, and healing.

Anger can only be released once it is healed through forgiveness, compassion, and empathy for self.

We can release the roots of anger by gently touching them with love.

finding peace and joy

May we all find inner peace, joy, happiness, and love. May we all seek to find understanding, compassion, and empathy for others and ourselves.

Our purpose here isn't to live in fear and angst, but to live a life that fills our hearts and satisfies our souls.

Life isn't meant to be complex. When we take it too seriously, we miss out on the gifts and opportunities we're given.

Find time for solace and serenity.

Admire the beauty and wonder of the world.

Peace and joy is within your reach.

Always be yourself, anything else
is dishonesty to the soul.
♥

frogs and snails and puppy-dogs' tails

Men have feelings, too. It's true, they really do.

Woman are wonderful creatures, often wearing our emotions on our sleeves for the world to see, and we tend to hold no shame or guilt for being vulnerable and free with our feelings.

Many men have been taught to hide their feelings. They've been told by mentors, friends, and fathers, that crying is a sign of weakness.

While it's difficult enough hearing it from other men, some woman carry the same ideals—a man should be stone, not soft, not in touch with their feelings.

Where does that leave men? Severely stressed, tight with tension, and often overcome by anxiety and depression.

We all know how it feels to have a good cry; it is a cleansing form of release.

If men are conditioned to believe crying is a *womanly* act, how do they find release? Anger, frustration, projection, or show no emotion at all.

When we encounter someone who doesn't express emotion towards us, either positive or negative, it can frustrate us. We unconsciously feel like they don't care about us. If they do care, they don't have the tools to express their emotions and show vulnerability without feeling like 'less of a man.'

What if men were encouraged to show their emotions? What if they were told it's okay to be vulnerable and real and cry if they need to? If we gave men *permission* to express their feelings in a safe space, then perhaps this would relieve the years of stress and tension they've been holding within, and thus, prevent future stress by opening doors to a new way of communication.

Some of the most amazing men I know show their sensitive side and are completely comfortable with showing emotion. I know these men to be healthy, strong, compassionate, and empathetic human beings. This is often referred to as a man's "feminine" side.

97

It should be their *natural* side.

Many men feel as though they are carrying the weight of the world on their shoulders. Unlike women, however, men don't often talk openly with their friends and family about how they're feeling. They just endure without expressing themselves in a healthy way, or at all.

A lot of men feel women can be very critical of them, which makes them close themselves. This could be why many a man's ego tends to be slightly more stubborn than the average woman's.

If you find your partner or loved one is uncomfortable with showing emotion or sharing their feelings, let them know you support them, that you're there to listen *without* judgment.

Avoid pointing fingers, blaming, or becoming defensive when communicating. Instead show compassion, empathy, and understanding.

Most importantly, be patience if the progress is slow. Not every man is eager or willing to pull down their walls and allow their feelings to show.

start by getting to know yourself

The best relationship you will ever have, is the relationship with yourself.

It's vital to understand and love yourself and to develop a strong sense of self-awareness and self-connection by getting to know *you*.

We at times can be too hard on ourselves, harshly judging our actions and inactions. Perhaps getting to know ourselves better, we will create a space of empathy, and we'll learn more about *who* we truly are.

Building a healthy relationship with yourself can be the foundation to creating healthy relationships with those around you.

Fall madly and deeply in love with yourself.

a lighter life

Life becomes *lighter* when you do more of what you love.

When you consciously choose who you spend time with and what you spend time doing, you become more aware of *who* you are, and *what* truthfully and honestly excites you.

Life becomes lighter when you begin to please your own heart and listen to the callings of your sweet soul.

Living lighter means letting go of what we don't need. It's releasing the baggage and burdens we carry upon our shoulders.

To live a lighter life, choose to love yourself more and honour the dreams that grow within your imagination.

you begin within

People wanting to live a more meaningful and purposeful life often ask themselves where to start their journey.

At first it may seem logical that your purpose can be found externally, somewhere tangible outside of yourself.

But it's not.

Your search for more purpose is found within your essence and in the quiet corners of your heart.

You just need to be still, and listen to what your soul is telling you.

Your search for more meaning, more purpose, and more peace is found within.

Start in the heart.

a sure man

A man is still a man if tears fill his eyes, for his tears consist of true compassion and love.

A man is not a coward because he *professes* his love, he is a man because he knows *how* to love.

His inner power does not want or need control, his power is projected through strength and support to his partner.

A sure man does not rely on attention from outside sources to affirm he is a man, he only needs a simple touch and a reassuring smile from his love, for this fills him with enough affirmation and contentment to carry him through the years.

Once he finds true love, a sure man is wise enough to acknowledge this precious gift, a gift that only those who believe in love will discover.

sensitive hearts

Do people say you're too sensitive, that you care too much, or get hurt too easily?

Sensitive beings who are easily affected by the emotions of others are often referred to as empaths. An empath is a person who can consciously and unconsciously tune in to the emotional experience of a person, place, or animal. The emotions they experience, whether "good" or "bad", can cause these individuals to feel happy and joyful or anxious and unsettled, depending on the situation.

When empaths are around people who are being less than authentic, in nature, they can feel uncomfortable and at a loss for words. They often avoid small talk and prefer not to watch movies or television shows that include violence. They feel physically sick when witnessing abuse to people and animals. They can withdraw immediately when confronted by someone who is angry or frustrated, and they often take things very personally and hold onto these feelings longer than others.

Sensitive people are very in touch with their feelings and in tune with their bodies. They know when something feels *off* and will typically only express their emotions with someone if they feel *safe*.

On the other hand, people seem to be drawn to sensitive and empathetic people. They feel an instant sense of safety and trust, and openly share deep emotional traumas they have experienced or are currently experiencing. You will find complete strangers being drawn to the energy of a empath. I believe it's an unconscious connection and inner knowing that the empath will understand and listen without judgment.

Because sensitive people have a heightened sense of the energies in their surroundings, many tend to withdrawal in social situations so they're not *exposed* or called upon. It is easier to hide at the back of the room than it is to be the centre of attention.

Being constantly aware of the emotions and energies of others can cause turmoil and anxiety, which can affect their own state of mind and well-being.

I personally have trouble in crowded locations like the mall or Walmart, as I find myself feeling anxious, unsettled, and even dizzy at times. You may find yourself unaffected by some locations, but troubled by others.

There are a few steps you can follow to protect yourself when in social situations or when you are feeling overcome with emotion:

- Seek out other sensitive souls who understand you. You're definitely not alone and you may learn from them how to better master and embrace your own sensitive super powers.
- Treat yourself with care and compassion. Understand you are a unique and loving individual who truly cares for the well-being of others; we need more people like you!
- Be mindful of what you put into your body. Conscious eating can be very important. Sugar, alcohol, and other stimulants tend to have a negative effect on sensitive/empathetic people.
- Don't hesitate to set boundaries to protect your nature. If you are not okay with something, communicate how you're feeling with certainty and confidence. Trust in yourself.
- Don't allow others to take advantage of you because of your loving and giving nature. Say 'no' when you need to. It's okay.
- Remember the pain of others is not yours. Be an observer, not an *absorber* of each experience.
- It is not always *your* feelings that you are feeling. Ask yourself, 'is this mine?' and listen for your answer. You'd be surprised how much this simple tool can help.
- And lastly, keep being *you*, the authentic beautiful you who holds a heart of love and hope. You are an individual who understands the importance of human connection and compassion.

self-love and acceptance

When you start to learn to love yourself, your self-worth magically becomes more valuable.

You begin to realize that you're worthy of happiness, healthy relationships, a fruitful career, or that dream you've yet to follow.

You are deserving of love and abundance. If you think you're not worthy, ask yourself why.

Go through the emotions and figure out what's blocking you from going after greatness.

You *do* deserve greatness, everyone does.

Seek it out and embrace it.

You are worth more than you realize. Never let anyone tell you otherwise.

One day you'll see how
brave and beautiful you really are.
And everything will change.
❤

believe in your beauty

Perhaps so many people aren't happy with their bodies and appearance because they've never taken the time to fully appreciate what they were given.

We all have our moments when we're unhappy with the way we look and, sometimes, those moments can last forever.

We focus on all the things we don't like about our bodies and fail to recognize the things we do like.

We never take time to see our own beauty. We shy away from compliments or brush them off. We think the person is lying or just being nice or maybe they want something. We find it difficult to believe someone sees us as beautiful, *truly* beautiful, and perhaps that's because we've convinced ourselves we're not.

We don't see it, so we don't believe it.

They say beauty is in the eye of the beholder, but it's often our own eyes that fail to see and appreciate our own inner and outer beauty.

Perhaps we need to spend more time looking at ourselves in the mirror, but not in the traditional sense.

We need to be honest and intimate with ourselves as we discover our beauty though our own eyes. We need to tell ourselves we're perfect just the way we are and, looking into our eyes and connecting with the person behind those eyes, open the windows to our soul.

Notice the lines, scars, and wrinkles and be okay with them instead of wishing them away. Be grateful they're there, for behind each one, is a story.

Our beautiful story.

By changing how we view our bodies, we'll come to appreciate them. By thanking our legs for helping us get around, our arms for allowing us to hug our loved ones, our eyes for providing us a chance to view our surroundings, we can then change how we see the world.

Instead of wishing we looked different, it is time to embrace who we are. That doesn't mean we shouldn't choose to exercise or do what we feel is right and healthy for us, it means we don't need to compare ourselves to others.

By accepting our *imperfections* we are free to fall absolutely and unconditionally in love with ourselves...every curve...every nook...every cranny.

I don't believe our *maker*, whoever that may be, intended for us to be "perfect". I think we're different by design; created in all colours and sizes, providing diversity and uniqueness.

So take a moment every day and get to know your body and love yourself inside and out.

By speaking to yourself using positive, loving, and gentle words rather than negative, hateful, and hurtful words, we'll come to a place where we can accept ourselves fully, and the need for the acceptance and approval of others will soon disappear.

You are beautiful, every single part of you, but don't take my word for it, take your own.

teach them how to love themselves

One of the most important lessons we can teach our children is the love of self.

Too often children hear their parents complain about their own bodies: they need to lose weight, gain weight, or change how they look. But how often do they hear parents complementing themselves and being completely happy with their appearance?

Do they hear words of confidence or insecurity?

Our self-talk, becomes their self-talk, and soon their minds become conditioned with negative thoughts.

By starting at home, with loving and accepting ourselves, our children will learn to love and accept themselves, and consciously and unconsciously it will become imbedded in the beliefs they carry throughout their lives.

If we want to nip one thing in the bud, we should be sure to nip that.

my soul calling

For many years in my life I felt empty in my heart, like something was missing, keeping it from feeling whole.

I knew it wasn't stemming from my relationship because I'd never been happier. I was following my passion for photography, creating art and memories for myself and for others, but still, something felt *off*.

After feeling this way for several months, I expressed this to my partner. I told him that there was something more that I was supposed to be doing but I didn't know what, only that it involved helping others. I truly *believe* we are all here to be of service to others.

I felt unsettled, not at ease with myself. My uncertainty bred my discontent. But I soon began listening to my heart stronger than before. I became more connected with the Universe and was more thankful for the abundance and love it had given me.

I started watching for the signs around me and, most of all, I listened to the calling of my soul. Because I sat still and listened to the whispers of my heart, I came to a place in my life of helping others heal, sharing inspiration, and giving my love freely and unconditionally.

When we connect within, with our mind, body, and spirit and trust the calling of our souls, we can live a life of humility and ease.

do you follow your intuition?

Our intuition acts as our internal guidance system, our source of inner wisdom and insight, and often *knows* things before our minds do.

That inexplicable sensation we all know could be considered our intuitive operating system. It sends us unconscious messages, often described as *gut feelings.*

We've all said: "I should've listened to my gut."

Many business leaders and professionals rely on the guidance of their intuition, basing their decisions on how they *feel* about a situation or circumstance, and do so successfully.

How many of us use our intuitive operating system in our day-to-day lives?

How would our lives be different if we listened to our intuition more and trusted what we feel?

We often overanalyze situations, observing from a place of logic, instead of listening to our internal voice.

I believe if we trusted more in our own capabilities and the power we hold within, our lives could be very different.

How does one tap into their intuition and use it at its full potential? Here are some suggestions.

~ **Quiet your mind**

> We are often so busy in our heads that the constant chatter overrides the act of being present, in the moment, or just being still. When we quiet our mind, we are able to hear our intuition above the chaos and noise.

~ **Meditate**

> If you're stuck on a decision, try mediation. Meditation isn't about stopping your thoughts, it's about slowing them down. Sometimes the answer is within the question, but we need to slow down our busy thoughts to receive our answer.

~ Journaling

When we journal our thoughts it awakens our creativity. When we connect with our creative energy it strengthens our intuition. The two go hand-in-hand. Try journaling a page a day, even if you don't know what to write.

~ Pay attention to your dreams, then write them down

Sometimes the answers we seek come to us in our dreams. It's a time for our unconscious thoughts to make an appearance. Journal your dreams when they seem profound and intense; they may carry the messages you need to hear.

~ Trust your gut

Your gut knows...I can't emphasize that enough. It's the inclination to take a different route from work, walk a different way home, or the unsettling feeling you get about a prospective client. It is your inner wisdom and guidance steering you clear. If something doesn't *feel* right, trust that feeling.

~ Step away from the situation

Don't feel like you must make a decision under pressure. If you aren't sure about something, step back, listen to the messages you are getting, and work from that place of peace and clarity. Then trust in your decision.

~ Remember to always be yourself

When you are your true authentic self, it gives yourself permission to be all you are and your intuition is a vital part of you. The more authentic you are in nature, the more confidence you gain in self, which allows you to connect with all levels of who you are, and what you are.

So next time you have a gut feeling about something, instead of passing it off, listen to it. And if you practice the suggestions above, you may find that you begin to run more on your intuitive operating system rather than only using logic for every situation. The more you trust your inner wisdom, the more you find you trust yourself.

breakdowns bring breakthroughs

Sometimes you have to become completely broken in order to feel whole again.

Every moment we experience brings us closer to finding who we're meant to be. It allows our true self to emerge from the comfortable cocoon we've nestled in for so long.

Avoiding pain and heartache only deters you from your path back to self.

Embrace every tear and every ounce of pain because nothing is gained by avoiding pain.

Push past what makes you feel weak and there you'll find your strength.

Trust the moment and surrender to its teachings.

Breakdowns can bring breakthroughs.

projected pain

You may not realize it at the time, but when others don't want to feel the pain they're experiencing they can project it upon you in an attempt to free themselves.

Pay attention when someone is pointing out your perceived flaws and faults; it is actually flaws and faults they see within themselves. However, by choosing to see these faults in you, rather them themselves, they are "free" from taking responsibility and making a change that could potentially be uncomfortable.

It can be difficult not to allow projected pain from others to hurt you, but accepting that hurt people hurt people can bring you solace and understanding.

The best advice I can give is to not take things too personally and forget about being offended, just keep focusing on your own success and happiness.

People who are happy and content within don't have time to waste energy and engage in drama, conflict or battles.

Rise up and rise on, and send love and healing to those who are hurting.

the energy we produce

It's interesting how negative and positive energy can affect *all* living things in your home.

I remember when I told my former partner that I was leaving our relationship. I hadn't been happy for years but I remained with him because I was afraid of what the future would bring my children and I.

A few days after I told him that I was leaving, he decided to buy me flowers; something he never did before. The next morning I awoke and came into our kitchen to find the flowers had died. These flowers were fresh and vibrant only the night before. They had fallen amongst the petals of each other and withered down the sides of the vase in a sad, but pretty pattern. They had no life left in them; the flowers resembled how I had been feeling for years.

The negative, angry, unhappy, and frustrated energy that flowed aimlessly throughout our house had killed the flowers. They absorbed the anger, the resentment, the sadness, and it killed them. They could not survive and thrive in an unhappy environment.

Much like humans.

The positive and negative energy we produce can be felt by all living things. You can feel it when you walk into a room. You just know that someone is angry or upset, and often times that person doesn't have to say a word for you to know. You just *feel* their anger, their unhappiness.

We should be mindful of our energy and how and where we place it. Because without knowing, it can be harmful to those around us and those we love.

Our children are often the ones who feel it the most, however, they don't always understand what they are feeling or why they are feeling it. They lack the ability to *express* it, so they *repress* it.

Once we become aware that everything around us is energy, we can become more conscious of the energy we produce.

Never focus on having a good reputation. Instead focus on the substance of your character. If you act with integrity, compassion, and kindness, your reputation will take care of itself.

♥

a higher frequency

People who reside on a lower frequency tend to complain, blame others for their lack of happiness, and often refuse to take responsibility for their own actions.

When residing on a lower energy frequency, it is easier for you to find the *negative* in most every situation because you will consciously and unconsciously seek it out.

People residing on lower frequencies often attract others who are on the same low vibrational frequency, and tend to believe "bad" things are happening to them all the time. Most who reside on this lower vibration don't even realize they are stuck in a negative place because it's become their way of life. Their mind has been conditioned.

How does one change their vibration to a higher frequency? By changing your mindset and becoming aware of your thoughts. Changing your state of mind, your choices, your perceptions, and in some cases, your environment.

Do this until you form a habit or until it becomes embedded in your conscious and unconscious belief system. When you're faced with a negative feeling, experience it, but instead of believing and accepting this lower thought, observe it and release it. Ask yourself, 'does this thought serve me purpose?' If the answer is 'no', it then becomes your conscious choice and responsibility if you decide to hold onto and believe the thought.

Emotional imbalances and past conditioning can cause you to operate on a lower energy frequency, but with healing, self-awareness, and mindful intentions, you can change your vibration.

Reiki, meditation, restorative yoga, therapy, energy work, clean eating, and removing yourself from toxic situations and people are only some of the wonderful and helpful methods to breathe positivity into your frequency.

lack of expression
leads to soul repression

When we choose to not express all that we are, we hide the very thing we need to be: ourselves.

Freedom is attained by being who you are, by shining your unique light, and sharing your authentic heart.

It's expressing through creativity, language, energy, and love.

It's allowing yourself to trust and listen to your intuitive gifts and communicate your truth with others, the Universe, and most importantly, yourself.

The most rewarding way to achieve freedom is through expression of the soul.

If you want to be free, you need to be you.

just be

Those "down" days, when you feel off, not right in your own skin, are the perfect days to allow yourself to just *be*.

It's a time to let yourself feel exactly how you're feeling without guilt or shame. It's a time for self-reflection, if desired, and it's a time to let your spirit *rest* if need be.

We can't always be happy.

We can't always be positive and "perfect".

We have to give ourselves space and time and permission to feel our emotions and let them encompass our being if they so wish to do so.

On your "off" days, do what your mind, body, and spirit requires. If that means doing nothing at all, then absolutely, do nothing at all.

you're good enough

Rejection can damage your self-esteem. It can make you feel worthless, unaccepted, not of value, and it can make you feel as though something is "wrong" with you.

But here's the thing—not everyone is going to connect with you or like you on the level you'd like them to. It just doesn't happen. It's not meant to happen.

When you show interest in a person but they don't show interest back, often your first thought is: did I say or do something wrong? Am I not pretty enough or good enough for them?

Key words here: "for them".

If you haven't learned to love and accept yourself, you will continue thinking something is wrong with you when others doesn't accept you.

When you place the value of yourself in the hands of others, you immediately give away your power.

When you learn to love and accept yourself and fully understand your own value and worth, you will begin to lose the desire to be "good enough" for everyone else.

This will create self-empowerment and soon you will no longer depend on the opinions and acceptance of others to define your worth.

Love yourself first and you won't need to be loved by everyone else.

no regrets

Some people spend their entire lives, never having truly lived.

Don't wait until it's too late and you're left looking back on your life with regret. Too often 'could've' and 'should've' leads to heartache or grief.

Live a life you can look back upon with contentment and personal satisfaction.

The moment you realize you live in a limitless Universe is the moment you begin to spread your wings and fly.

Live your life to the fullest.

Do the things you love.

Tell people you love them.

Eat cake.

Stay up late.

Get up early.

Watch a sunset.

Watch a sunrise.

Be the reason someone smiles today.

Don't wait for tomorrow.

getting what you 'deserve'

We unconsciously seek what we believe we deserve.

This is often true in relationships, careers, our own self-love.

But why do we sometimes think we are unworthy of greatness?

Were we not told as children to never settle for less than we deserve? Were we not told that we're worthy of greatness, healthy love, and happiness?

I've been in a handful of relationships where I settled for mediocre. Yet I hoped the person would change into who I *wanted* and *needed* them to be.

I imagined that one day they would be everything I dreamed of, even though I knew, in my heart, where my truth lies, it would never happen. Still I waited, sometimes for years, for something to change.

I endured sadness, heartache, frustration, anger, resentment. I cried more than I laughed. I tried to make it work. But it wasn't meant to work long term, no matter how many tears I cried.

Relationships take work. They take remarkable amounts of effort, commitment, and communication, but shouldn't take the kind of *work* that consists of constant fighting, pain, and heartache.

When long-term relationships come to end, those involved are often judged for not trying "hard enough". But what if one or both weren't aware of what they deserved, and it took that relationship to make them aware? Maybe their intentions were good. Perhaps they tried to make it work but their feelings changed. That's something none of us can control.

I strongly believe people come into our lives for a reason. Sometimes they stay for a very short period of time. And that's okay. Not everything is meant to last forever. We need certain people in our lives to teach us the hard lessons that activate and enhance our spiritual growth. Sometimes we need *unhealthy* love to push us towards unearthing *healthy* love.

I lived so many years dying inside because I didn't know I was worthy of greatness.

But I'm grateful for my past relationships, as they served me much purpose. Regardless of how painful the path could be at times, it eventually lead me to peace.

Be grateful for the people who ended relationships with you. Be thankful for the ones you left.

You may have felt anger, resentment, sadness, and even hate for them, but are you happy now?

Are you in a new relationship or on your own?

Thank that person for giving you the opportunity to find love again and the opportunity to love yourself.

We're all worthy of good, healthy love.

The unhealthy love or "loveless" relationships we've endured were needed to help awaken us, to awaken our needs and our wants.

Sometimes when a relationship ends, it feels like *the* end.

But it's really only the beginning.

When a flower dies, another one grows from its seed.

it's okay to change

If you ever find yourself re-evaluating your current relationships or friendships, chances are you are experiencing a shift.

Don't feel badly about it.

Some people require friendships/relationships filled with substance and meaning, relationships that make them feel valued and appreciated. If that is what you require, then you shouldn't feel badly about it. It doesn't mean that particular friendship or relationship needs to come to an end. Maybe it means things will be a little different moving forward. Different is sometimes better.

Do what feels good for *you*. You're not being selfish. In fact you're being quite the opposite.

Listen to that little voice whispering in your heart, asking for change.

It always knows what's best.

change of heart

If you are in a relationship and feel as though you rarely see eye-to-eye, that nothing's easy, then perhaps your vibrations are no longer aligning and resonating with each other.

Your energy isn't *always* going to vibrate on the same frequency as those close to you. And this can cause conflict, frequent disagreements, and perhaps resentment because your partner "just doesn't get you".

We often try to make relationships work because we believe it would be easier if they did. It might be time to accept what you can't change. It also may mean it is time to let go.

Relationships can be beautiful. They are our teachers. We learn and grow from them. However, sometimes a relationship serves its purpose and it's time to move on, start a new chapter. This is not something you should feel guilty about or be afraid of.

It can also be a time to explore together a new way to remain in the relationship by setting healthy boundaries and communicating and understanding each other on a deeper level.

Whatever you decide to do, ensure your decisions and actions are based on what your heart is telling you.

the secret

There's no "secret" when it's comes to attaining abundance, happiness, and success. There is no ancient mystery that only a lucky few uncover.

When you consider your dreams to be surreptitious, you instantly create boundaries and obstacles; you consciously and unconsciously view your dreams as unattainable. Because if there's a chance of failure, why bother trying, right?

Refrain from harboring the mindset that success is only for the chosen few. It is not. It's available to everyone and, if you believe, you can receive.

Everything you need to succeed is inside you. It's in your thoughts, your imagination, your energy, your heart, your creations. All the bricks to build your dreams are already at hand. You possess the tools you need to succeed.

You are the creator of your destiny, the builder of your desires.

If you want to achieve success, it's necessary you have a clear vision of your destination. A ship doesn't leave the port without knowing where it's headed.

The secret to success is no secret at all.

Success is achieved by belief, choice, and hard work.

happiness and freedom

I have always loved the saying: "once you go within, you will never go without".

I spent years seeking happiness from external sources. I searched for it in relationships, in friendships, and in material belongings. But nothing ever brought me happiness, *organic* happiness, that comes without prompting from anything at all.

I felt this way until one day I awoke and everything I believed to be true came crashing down. The world I once perceived to be real, was anything but. When I started discovering the truth of the world, or what I now perceived to be the truth, my life changed in an instant, with no warning, and it was scary and painful at times.

It forced me to look inwardly and see where changes could be made. This self-reflection and self-discovery was the start of my journey to happiness and freedom.

I used to blame others for what happened *to* me. I lacked the understanding that things were happening *for* me. They were life lessons, given to me.

They were a gift. A chance to learn.

I had to repeat these lessons until I learned them. I had to start taking responsibility for my actions and my choices, and take ownership of what I put out into the Universe.

We attract what we are. If I was unhappy and feeling worthless, I would unconsciously seek others who felt the same.

Once my mindset changed, my life changed.

I starting seeing the world in a new light—a bright, clear light. The heavy responsibility of expecting to find happiness from others soon left me and I felt free, truly free.

I experienced many roller coaster moments because I was now in charge of making myself feel better in moments of hurt, of pain, and of anger.

I had to find within my own being the strength to push past the pain, while allowing myself to feel the pain. But I refused to let it become me, to define me. I had to release the role of being a victim and accept the role of being a survivor, a warrior.

My awakening was a gift. A gift of insight, of wisdom, and the strong ability to use and to trust my own intuition. It was the gift of the rebirth of my true self.

I'm forever thankful and grateful for the day I awoke to realize I had been "sleeping" most my life.

Your passions are your purpose.
Trust the calling you feel within,
it beholds something special.

♥

spirituality

Spirituality cannot be defined nor described, it's felt through experiences of the soul. It's a journey of lessons and love, pain and sorrow.

It is rare moments so utterly real it evokes a profound and intense emotion, followed by a deep understanding and connection to others, to the Universe, and to self.

Spirituality cannot be reached via plane or train, it cannot be taught over the internet or in a book with folded pages and torn binds. It can only be reached by travelling within oneself. Travelling solo to the depths of the darkest places that you once feared to venture.

Spirituality is reconnecting to the very essence of your being. It's going home, where the heart awaits with patience and perseverance, and without judgment and conditions.

Spirituality is knowing on an unconscious level that the Universe has its best intentions for you.

It is being one with oneself in the moment while listening to the gentle whispers of your boundless soul.

shine without shame

One of the most beautiful processes in life is unbecoming the person we thought we *had* to be and becoming the person we were *meant* to be.

We start to truly live when we remove our masks and burn the veils that have kept us separate from others, and from ourselves for far too long.

When we awaken within and choose to expose our authenticity to the world, we are consciously choosing to share who we are and shine without shame.

Becoming who we were meant to be, is truly the greatest gift of all.

inspired action

Action really is everything.

Without action our dreams continue their slumber.

Without action our true desires are never realized.

Without action the life we want will remain forever elusive.

Without action we cannot be our best.

Always believe you can achieve and receive what you wish.

But believing is not enough.

Inspired action is required to transform your belief into physical reality.

Dream, plan, act, enjoy.

you get out of life what you are

If you want to achieve greater success, surround yourself with people who inspire, support, and encourage you. Surround yourself with the ones who lift you up when you've fallen down.

Pay no mind to the ones who talk behind your back, the ones who speak words of negativity. Those who do this are unconsciously expressing their own insecurities. People who are confident and secure, self-assured and wise, find no need to point out "flaws" in others. They are too focused on their own success to give their energy to sabotage another.

The true determined and successful individual wakes up inspired. They rise and they shine. They push, they give, and they get. They focus, they plan, they dream, and they create.

There is one guarantee in life: if you don't take action, there will be no outcome. This is not the time to fear mistakes. Mistakes can often be the fuel to your success.

Be so positive that it pushes out the negative—you attract what you are. If you want to attract greatness, be great, think great things, be around great people.

You get in life what you *are.*

take a bite out of life

The guilt we often feel when doing something we think we "shouldn't" do doesn't always derive from internal conflict, but from external sources.

Although self-discipline is important, it's just as important to relish in all the little things in life that feed our happiness.

Life is to be lived in balance and harmony. So have the chocolate, enjoy the glass of wine, stay in bed all day if you want.

Just don't be so hard on yourself.

your only competition...is you

There will always be others doing what you're doing, selling what you're selling, offering the same service you offer.

But they are *not* your competition.

You are your competition.

Don't try to be better than others, try to be better than who you were yesterday.

The ultimate key to your success is not how much money you spend in marketing or advertising, it's not how many network events you attend, or how many people you reach out to. The ultimate key to your success is your authenticity.

It's how you make people feel when they're around you, and how they feel after they have left your presence.

It's your candid ability to make someone feel important, safe, and respected. It's the manner in which you communicate with others, how you listen and understand their requests and concerns.

The key to your success is remaining authentic and real and by leading with love.

Success is not found outside of yourself, it's found within your heart.

i am only but a soul

I am a mother, a partner, a sister, a daughter, a lover, a friend, a business owner, a caretaker, a helper, a creator.

I am many things.

Beneath all my labels, all my titles, and underneath the layers of my skin, wrapped around my bones, you will find my soul.

Our souls are made of energy and love. They carry us through the day, never giving up on us.

Before your soul changes its state, it's your responsibility to connect, re-connect with your true self, where no words could ever define who you ultimately are: a being of love and light.

We are here to love and teach each other. We are here to love and teach ourselves.

It's our birthright and unconscious need to share our truth.

Underneath it all, we are only but a soul. A soul who wants to soar.

Surrendering ends suffering,
letting go of what was,
allows you to appreciate what is.
And what is, is all we have.

♥

what does surrender mean to me?

Surrender means releasing pain, attachments, fear, guilt, beliefs—anything that holds you back from growing, changing, evolving, and experiencing new things.

We try to hold on to past emotions, fears, guilt, and traumas because we think they define us. We believe we need to carry these burdens around with us because they tell our story. Yes, they *do* tell part of our story, but they can also keep you stuck in the same chapter for years if you don't learn to turn the page and let them go.

You are not defined by your past. Holding on to pain and anger causes stress within your body; that stress can turn into disease of many forms.

Are you often tired, sick, stressed, angry, and worried for reasons you can't quite pinpoint? Past pain remains present in the body for as long as you allow it. This pain is often deferred into other areas of your body and your *emotional* pain can result in *physical* pain.

Try being alone with yourself. Sit quietly and listen to your body, feel the sensations, reconnect with yourself. Walk in nature and be in awe of its beauty. Don't live in your past. Doing so can make you forget about living in the present.

You must learn to surrender and release emotions that no longer serve you. If you want to experience true freedom of the heart, then you must clear your heart of the old to allow for all the new that awaits.

The more you let go, the higher you fly.

Every time you re-live a negative feeling and emotion from your past, you re-live the unpleasant feelings. The more you do this, the more moments of pain and suffering you experience. Holding on will only hinder your growth and personal progress.

Let go, forgive yourself, and forgive those who've hurt you.

Surrender to what was and rejoice in what is.

a balanced ego is a healthy ego

You may think you don't have an ego, but everyone does.

Your ego is a part of who you are and, when in balance, it can be a good thing.

Our ego drives our desire to look good, professional, presentable. Without it, we simply wouldn't care. It can drive us to success, achieve what we want in life, help build our confidence, and remind us that we are good enough. Ego also inspires a leader's ability to take charge and to take initiative.

But when your ego is not in balance, it can cause you to be insecure, judgmental, and unforgiving. You are quick to judge others and you feel inferior to them. You engage in frequent drama, gossip, and point out what you perceive to be "wrong" in others. You have a belief that you're better than everyone and don't like seeing others succeed, even your own friends or family. Ego can also be stubborn and doesn't forgive easily, or at all.

So how do you balance your ego to a healthy state?

Give up the need to be right and listen to others. It is said that when engaged in conversation, it's important to listen 80 percent of the time and speak 20 percent of the time. Encourage and support others, and applaud their successes.

Be aware if your ego is fragile or confident. Do you get hurt and offended easily or do you stay high in self-confidence and self-awareness? Develop the ability to better understand others. Ask questions, be curious of those around you, and be interested in what others do. Practice forgiveness and letting go.

Your ego is a key to your self-awareness. When we release control and any denial of who we are, it offers an interesting and new feeling of freedom.

If you want to work on balancing your ego, first understand your ego exists.

Acknowledgment and responsibility create change.

giving up

I give up my worries and fears that take away from my inner peace and effect my outer presence.

I give up toxic relationships that bring me down rather than lift me up.

I give up dispersing my energy where right now, it isn't needed.

I give up trying to control what was never mine to control.

I give up worrying about *what if* and I choose to delight in *what is.*

I give up trying to be perfect in an imperfect world.

I give up the thoughts that mock me, the ones that devalue my self-worth.

I give up the troubles that consume me, and surrender them to the sky.

I give up the doubts that haunt me, the illusions of my mind.

I give up what doesn't serve me or evolve my spiritual growth.

I give up all that isn't, and allow all that is.

power of no

One of the most powerful words there is contains only two letters.

No.

I have always felt as though I *had* to say 'yes' to everything and everyone. I would take part in situations that did not align with my interests and I would invest my time and energy where I didn't want to invest it, simply to please others.

I would feel guilty if I didn't.

But soon that guilt changed into resentment.

Why do we feel guilty for saying no? What has conditioned us to feel this way? Is it because we're so worried about how the other person will feel? If they feel upset, angry, or disappointed, then *we* feel bad. We don't want to feel bad, so we do what we can to avoid it.

It is important to understand that our guilt is our choice. No one can *make* us feel guilty. They may be upset, but that's them choosing to feel upset.

Emotions don't need to be involved. Say 'no' and carry on.

Try 'no' on for size. I bet it will fit just right.

spend your time wisely

Time is far too precious to waste it, so choose wisely how you use it.

Spend time with yourself, family, and good friends. Spend it doing something you love.

When you give your time and energy to people and situations that don't expand and enhance your energy and soul growth, you can become depleted, exhausted, and left feeling empty.

How do you want to spend your time and energy?

Invest it in people and things that help raise your vibration to a higher and more positive frequency.

Because time is truly of the essence, spend it wisely.

triggers trigger truth

When a person, situation, image, or word *triggers* you, you may feel a number of unpleasant feelings, including anger. This can cause you to react defensively.

We deflect the feelings we're experiencing upon others in order to not face the triggering emotion. However, when we do this, we deny ourselves an opportunity for self-reflection. Our ego does not want us to believe there's something "wrong" with us.

But triggers trigger truth.

Sometimes that truth can be an ugly truth. If something upsets you easily, it's often because a similar situation happened at some point in your life that caused an emotional reaction and a feeling of pain. It's embedded in your cellular memory. Therefore, when this old emotion is triggered and brought back to the surface, you do everything in your power to push it back down and hide it.

Instead of rejecting and projecting upon others, explore and experience your feelings and ask yourself why this may be returning to the surface. What are the feelings wanting you to see?

You might find by facing your triggered feelings, even the uncomfortable and painful ones, you will find inner healing and resolution.

Sometimes the truth can be painful, but often times we need pain in order to grow. You've been there before and those painful situations led you to where you are today.

Triggers trigger truth, and they can also trigger growth.

my vulnerable heart

I can pretend to always be strong, but the truth is, I'm not.

I have moments of insecurity and doubt, moments when I lack self-worth and confidence.

I have times when my vulnerable side is showing more skin than I'd prefer.

I have unexpected moments when I hurt, experience disappointment, and feel uncertain about all things.

And in those unexpected moments I may cry, withdraw, and quietly scream for attention.

I don't avoid feeling pain. Sometimes I *need* it, I invite it in. Pain can create change.

I am not one to shame myself for expressing my dismay, for I understand that my emotions should be acknowledged, embraced, and cared for.

Like all moments, they too will pass.

I can pretend to always be strong, but the truth is, I'm not.

rising above

I'm intrigued by those who speak their words from a place of truth, a place of experience, and a place of persistency.

I'm inspired by their determination to beat the odds, their aspiration, and their ability to surrender to what is.

The most meaningful words that ever hit my heart were the words of someone's beautiful truth that arose from the deepest parts of them. I admire the ones who, despite all their setbacks and all their years of trauma and tragedy, choose to shine.

They survived the obstacles that tried to push them off their path. They got back onto their feet with grace and resilience, and with a gift a wisdom to share.

To rise from the ashes with hope in one's heart is true bravery at its finest.

shine light onto your darkness

There was a time when I was young, vulnerable, and in love. My self-esteem was low, I had no self-worth, and found myself in an abusive relationship.

I recall one particular incident when my back had been scratched after being pushed into a pane of glass by my former partner. I remember thinking as he cleaned the blood from the cuts, 'this is so nice of him'.

When you're in an abusive relationship you hold on to the "nice" things they do for you and convince yourself they'll change into the person you desperately want them to be. You minimize the abuse and live in denial, which sadly becomes easier every day; time tends to lessen the intensity of your experiences.

I understand now that hurt people hurt people. Yes, he was hurting, but so was I.

Years of abuse almost broke my spirit. I had forgotten who I was because the pain became a part of my everyday life. I was simply existing.

Eventually I gathered my "broken" pieces with hope in my heart that I could make myself whole again.

I never told anyone about what was happening. For reasons I didn't understand, I feared painting an ugly picture of him. Perhaps I felt like it would reflect poorly on me.

When I finally did leave him, it took me time to re-learn how to love myself.

I believe it's important we share the vulnerable side of us because it's our vulnerabilities and our stories that connect our souls.

Our stories remind us that we are not alone.

I don't share my words from a place of pain, but from a place of purpose. If I never experienced the darkness, I would have never found my light.

We can banish our shadows by exposing them to light.

be in the moment

If you find your thoughts drifting into a dark space, bring yourself back to the moment by changing your focus and going within.

To feel truly in the moment, connect to your sensations. Feel the tingling in your hands and feet, feel the energy as it runs effortlessly throughout your entire body, and become conscious of the sounds around you.

Be alert of your surroundings.

If you want to change your thoughts, change your focus, and focus within.

Consciously connect to your being by acknowledging your presence in the only moment that truly exists.

*There are blessings to be found
in the bellies of our burdens.*

♥

your best work comes from love

When you put your heart into your work, people feel that love.

Working from a place of love results in a different kind of energy, an energy that originates from an authentic and organic place, a place of passion and compassion.

You touch others more deeply when you truly care about what you do, and how you do it.

Your best work always comes from that which you love.

set those feelings free

Forgiveness releases pain and makes room for new love and growth.

Imagine how it would feel to release your grasp on your resentment, your hurt, your anger. Imagine how it would feel to let go of the things that still cause you pain.

Forgiveness is not given for the sake of someone else's heart, but for the sake and sanity of your own.

When we forgive, we give ourselves room to breathe, to feel alive.

Holding onto our emotions is like locking them behind bars. The good news is, you hold the key to set them free.

Begin with forgiveness for self and let go of any emotions that hinder your ability to move onward and upward.

just listen

The best thing we can do as humans is to listen to others. To open our compassionate hearts and our empathetic souls, and listen with open ears.

Many times people are not seeking answers or opinions from others, but understanding and a sense of safety.

They're searching for someone to hear the soft cries of their spirit when it feels broken and alone.

They want reassurance that everything will be okay.

We need to give to those what they are desperately seeking so we can help guide them towards a valley of temporary relief from their emotional despair.

In our fruitless attempt to overturn our own suffering, it is the attention of others that will help bring us respite. Even if it's only for a moment.

We tell our stories to others in hopes of finding peace.

see your fears

Don't bury your fears so deep that they never see the light.

Feel them, express them, flaunt them to the world if you need to, for this is how we set them free—by exposing them to the light and facing them with bravery and boldness and determination.

Our fears try to protect us. They try to save our hearts and souls from experiencing trauma and tragedy.

However, by hiding our fears and burying them deep inside only gives them the room to grow.

We can release our fears by acknowledging them and seeing them for what they are.

Each time we face a fear, it gives us an opportunity to overcome it.

setting boundaries

Setting healthy boundaries is important. It lets a person know what is acceptable behavior and what is not.

If you find you're continually being taken advantage of or "walked over", then perhaps it's time to set new boundaries.

Give yourself permission to be clear and concise about what behavior you feel is acceptable. Get in touch with your feelings and core values, and ask yourself to distinguish what is healthy and what is not in regards to your relationships and friendships.

Don't be afraid to be direct with others. People treat us how we teach them to treat us. If we want to be treated otherwise, we must teach them differently.

You will create healthy and fruitful connections once you establish and implement boundaries. This can prevent future situations that cause turmoil, tension, and grief.

Healthy boundaries create healthy connections.

you're not broken

Have you ever felt broken, like you couldn't go on?

Have you felt defined by your past or the burdens you bear?

You may feel or have felt broken, but I promise you, you're not.

Underneath the shattered pieces of your spirit, remains your true essence: your soul, your beauty, your love, and that cannot be broken.

What *can* feel broken is your heart, your perception of how you see yourself, and your ability to give and receive love.

When pain is inflicted upon us, and when we have experienced trauma and years of neglect from self and others, we can be left feeling numb to the world and or highly sensitive to our environments.

When we choose, however, to see ourselves as whole, and gather the strength to pick up the pieces and mend our own hearts, we soon discover that what remains is the perfect essence of who we are.

I experienced different forms of abuse in past relationships. I felt lost, broken, and torn apart at the heart. What was broken was my perception of what healthy love was, and I had never felt more alone in my life. When I couldn't see the light, I listened to the voice that reassured me of better things to come.

'You're going to be okay, I promise'.

I was always whole. Inside. I was always *me*, even when I perceived myself as broken, lost, and utterly alone.

You can't break what you're born with. Love—your gift at birth. Love is who you are.

It's a matter of digging deep, excavating your own soul, and removing the years of stored anguish. It's looking beneath all the layers of hurt and under all the masks you wore with a painted smile.

When you've finally become tired of the pain and decide to accept what no longer is, is the day you'll find your unbroken pieces.

You'll return to love that day.

You'll understand you were never really broken, you were only temporarily separated from your heart.

I wish that day, that moment for anyone who has felt or feels broken. I wish you the rediscovery of who you are, the person who was never really broken.

sweet little things

I rejoice in the simpler pleasures life has to offer, like cool misty mornings when half the world is still asleep or the way the moonlight dances upon the water like tiny fireflies.

My morning cup of tea and the solitude it provides.

The sound of rain on the window on a summer's night.

These are the moments that hold the sweetest joy for me. These are the moments that contain the most peace.

Simple moments such as these allow us to appreciate the beauty life has to offer.

When we observe the beauty found in the *small* things, they become the *big* things, filling us with bliss, contentment, and gratitude.

I love the sweet little things in life, for they bring me my biggest joy.

The more we let go,
the more grace we let in.
♥

dream and dance along your path

Follow the path that feels right, the one that resonates with the truth of your soul.

Pay no attention to the opinions of others, this is *your* journey of adventure, self-discovery, and love.

Walk with integrity, passion, and compassion, and remain light at heart.

Dream what you dare, dance while you can, and do what you love.

And if you ever think something is impossible, remember you were once stardust and you made it this far.

You're here.

If *you* are possible, *anything* is possible.

the ones who feel like home

Have you ever spent time with people who you feel are judging you?

People who, no matter how hard you try, you just don't seem to connect or relate with them. Small talk doesn't even do the trick. It just feels uncomfortable and inauthentic. You find yourself watching the clock, itching to escape so you can breathe again.

And then you meet people who you connect with in an instant.

There's just an inner familiarity, like you've known them all along. They accept and embrace you, they see you for all that you are, and all that they don't know quite yet.

Their presence and energy feels safe, honest, and real.

In the grand scheme of things, we're really not here that long. Time does its thing and passes in the blink of an eye, and it doesn't look back.

So it's important to spend that time with the people you love and the ones who love you, with those who appreciate and understand you, and the ones who really *see* you.

We will never regret time well spent with the ones who feel like home.

our pain holds our wisdom

It's our pain and scars that bring us our wisdom.

It's the hard times and the lessons we receive that help us grow, that help us understand, and help us better love ourselves and others.

It's the storms that help us appreciate the sun even more.

It's the tragedies of the world that encourage us to hold our loved ones a little bit longer, and a whole lot tighter.

It's the battles we witness that give us courage in times of heartache and despair.

If it wasn't for our times of sadness and our moments of agony, we would cease to change, and a life without change would be quite a shame.

It's during our deep moments of weakness and feeling like we can't go on that we discover the well of strength flowing within us.

Our challenges bring us growth, our heartaches bring us progression, and if we don't shine light on our shadows, we ultimately deny the very parts of us that long for the most love.

The parts of us that feel the most pain, behold the most wisdom.

failure brings growth

We fail so we can experience what earned success feels like.

We fail so we can understand what we need to do, so we can do better.

We fail so we can appreciate the benefits of hard work.

We fail so we can become more empowered, yet humble at heart.

We fail so we can learn what doesn't work and what needs to be done to make it more successful.

Failure develops growth, and growth is necessary for greater success.

*Align your journey with
your truth, the road becomes
resistant when it's not aligned
with your heart.*

- ♥

live from the inside out

Share from your heart center, from the truth of your soul.

Express your energy from your authentic core, from your genuine and true essence.

Do not fear showing others who you are, just be *what* you are, and *who* you are, especially if it feels good and right for you.

When we live and work from the inside out, the opportunities and miracles that present themselves in our lives appear almost too good to be true.

But they're not.

They are what happens when we consciously choose to align ourselves with who we are. Miracles happen when we do the things we love.

When you live from the inside out, you experience the magic that awaits you when you let go of who you thought you were and become who you were meant to be.

Who you always were.

where do our dreams fit in?

What do you love? What fills you with ecstasy and excitement? What makes you lose track of time? What makes you lose track of yourself? What makes your heart sing?

We often find ourselves wondering how we arrived at this place and space in time, wondering who we are and where we went. We question where our dreams have gone and how they escaped our hearts without a sound nor trace of the magic we once held so dearly.

It's life. Life gets in the way of our dreams, our desires, and of our truth.

We work away our days, waiting for them to end, only to begin and end again. Each day that falls behind us is just another day that we swim through the rough waters without our dreams in tow. We leave them behind at the shore, only to be washed away by the tides, to be lost among the salty sands.

Is it the roles we take: husband, wife, mother, father? Is it the stress of life that rips our dreams so abruptly from our hearts? Or is it the expectations others place upon our backs that make us put aside what we love? Do we let go of *who* we are to become *what* others want us to be?

The importance of doing something you love is as vital as the air we breathe. It's a necessity, it's how we thrive, how we feel alive. It literally pours within our cells a feeling of pure bliss and happiness, and it's what makes our heart beat faster when we're engaged in the moments of doing what our soul seeks.

Doing something you love doesn't have to be a career, it doesn't have to take up your whole day if you don't want it to, but it should fit into your day like any other important task.

What if you're not passionate about something? How do you find out what moves your heart?

You play, create, invent.

Be curious, try as many new things as you can. Take ideas and sit with them, and then run with them. Maybe it's helping others within your community or a friend redecorate their home. If you look long and hard enough, you will find what sets your soul ablaze.

Your dreams and passions lay dormant until you do something to awaken them. Sometimes the thing we love is only a song or painting away.

We aren't here to work our lives away, we are here to revel in all the gifts we were given, and embrace the treasures that were born within us.

We're here to bask in the brilliance of life before we pack up our souls and leave this place for good.

Take the time to discover or rediscover what you love.

Nothing can bring you more happiness then sharing what you love with the world.

never stop shining

Never be afraid to shine.

Don't hide your magic from the world.

Your light is a beacon for others in their moments of darkness and despair.

You're a breath of fresh air for those who feel they can't breathe away the worries of the world.

You're just like home to someone.

We often dull our shine to appease the ones who are uncomfortable with what we radiate when we share from our authentic hearts. But when you choose not to shine you withhold what the world needs more of.

Love.

Compassion.

Empathy.

Kindness.

You aren't here to live amongst the shadows, to hide in the corners of discontent and mediocrity, you're here to offer your heart with love and to save the hearts of others, so they too can find their light.

heart is where the home is

You grow into the person you were meant to be while in pursuit of your passions.

Your true self comes alive when you align with your dreams, when you choose to carve your own path, and design your own rules to live by.

The more you follow the callings of your heart, the more you become who you're meant to be, who you always were, before time and experiences changed you.

One day you will awake feeling more like yourself than ever before. That is the day you'll find yourself home, home within the heart, and you'll discover that heart *is* where the home is.

We must recognize others
for the souls they are.
For the evolution of mankind,
we need to look deeper than what
the eye can see, and go beyond
what the mind can fathom.
♥

Thank you for taking time to read the musings of my soul.

I don't for one moment expect, think, or even hope you'll agree with all the truths I hold.

One truth is for certain, however—we all have the free will to believe what we choose, and no one is right or wrong in their beliefs; it's a matter of perception.

Strive each day to listen to others with understanding and without judgment, and carry kindness in your heart.

I encourage you to connect with me. I would love to hear about your trials, tribulations, and triumphs.

We're in this journey together.

You are not alone.

vanessamariedewsbury@gmail.com

www.vanessamariedewsbury.com

IG: vanessamariedewsbury

FB: Vanessa Marie Dewsbury

Twitter: @ASoulAlive

about the author

Vanessa Marie Dewsbury is a Spiritual Life Coach, Reiki Master, and Amazon Best Selling Author living in Barrie, Ontario, Canada.

Inspired by her health issues in 2012, Vanessa began her journey of natural healing after unsuccessful attempts to find answers through Western medicine.

She eventually found relief through natural healing therapies such as acupuncture, meditation, yoga, and natural herbs.

By connecting within and addressing old wounds, she was able to release and heal what was unconsciously affecting her health emotionally, mentally, and physically.

This internal shift not only healed her health issues but it awakened a well of wisdom and new found perspective on life, which she now shares freely with those around her.

Made in the USA
Middletown, DE
03 July 2019